# BEFORE THE PIONEERS

*Florida in Focus*

## UNIVERSITY PRESS OF FLORIDA

Florida A&M University, Tallahassee
Florida Atlantic University, Boca Raton
Florida Gulf Coast University, Ft. Myers
Florida International University, Miami
Florida State University, Tallahassee
New College of Florida, Sarasota
University of Central Florida, Orlando
University of Florida, Gainesville
University of North Florida, Jacksonville
University of South Florida, Tampa
University of West Florida, Pensacola

# BEFORE THE PIONEERS

Indians, Settlers, Slaves, and the Founding of Miami

ANDREW K. FRANK

University Press of Florida
Gainesville · Tallahassee · Tampa · Boca Raton
Pensacola · Orlando · Miami · Jacksonville · Ft. Myers · Sarasota

This book may be available in an electronic edition.

22 21 20 19 18 17  6 5 4 3 2 1

Library of Congress Control Number: 2017931108
ISBN 978-0-8130-5451-3

The University Press of Florida is the scholarly publishing agency for the State
University System of Florida, comprising Florida A&M University, Florida Atlantic
University, Florida Gulf Coast University, Florida International University, Florida
State University, New College of Florida, University of Central Florida, University of
Florida, University of North Florida, University of South Florida, and University of
West Florida.

 University Press of Florida
15 Northwest 15th Street
Gainesville, FL 32611-2079
http://upress.ufl.edu

In memory of and in honor of my grandparents:
Shirley and Samuel Frank, Sylvia and Daniel Klein,
Shirley and Jack Seitlin, and Helen and Isadore Tendrich

# CONTENTS

# FIGURES

# BEFORE THE PIONEERS

# INTRODUCTION

## MIAMI'S LOST HISTORY

I T IS AN ANCIENT PLACE that history has forgotten. Surrounded by
steel, glass, concrete, water, and millions of residents from across
the globe, the taproot of the North Bank of the Miami River may
be difficult to imagine. Yet the location connects modern Miamians,
Floridians, and Americans more broadly to an ancient world and
peoples. Nestled along scenic Biscayne Bay and a Miami River that
drains out of the Everglades, the location has endured for many millennia to become the centerpiece of south Florida development. For
around 4,000 years, the North Bank of the Miami River has been a
continuous meeting place and home for various peoples in the region. Its distinctive setting with many advantageous natural features
lured a diversity of residents that included Tequesta Indians, Spanish missionaries, African slaves, Seminole Indians, Bahamian boat-
ers, wartime refugees, merchants, planters, developers, and tourists.
Although residents straddled both sides of the river for many years,
sustained and enduring development largely focused on the North
Bank. It offered residents a set of advantageous natural features even
if the inhabitants never gave the peculiar location a proper name. The
North Bank—as this volume terms the locale—had a high ridge overlooking the bay, waterfront connections to the Caribbean and Atlantic

worlds, riverine ties to the inland Everglades, the bounty of the tropical ecology, and a temperate climate. The site even had access to fresh
water through the Miami River and a natural spring, providing locals
with that precious commodity.[1]

Not content with its natural advantages, the ancient Tequestas created the first of a series of human-made improvements that further
attracted visitors to the site and put the North Bank on dozens of
early European maps. Many of these physical alterations—especially
those to the natural world—went unnoticed. Julia Tuttle, for example, lauded the "wild" lime trees that Bahamian sailors had planted
a century or two earlier. Other modifications, however, could not be
ignored. The area's subsequent occupants took advantage of several
long-lasting buildings, a durable coral rock wall, a human-made well,
and abandoned supplies that included watercraft, lumber, tools, and
food. Together, these traits and improvements sustained the site's
occupants and linked it to the major themes and developments in
Florida history.

*Before the Pioneers* synthesizes this unique history. Although the
site is relatively small—measured in hundreds of square acres rather
than in square miles—the North Bank played an oversized role in
the development of the region. For as long as four thousand years,
the site has stood at the center of the human history of south Florida.
Other early American sites (Jamestown, Plymouth Rock, St. Augustine) certainly have a more important and visible place in the American and regional narrative. Cahokia in Illinois was a significantly
larger ancient Indian civilization than the Indian village on the North
Bank. The Apalachee Indians in the Florida panhandle had a much
longer history with Catholicism than did the Tequestas. Florida and
every other slaveholding state contained plantations that were larger,
more profitable, and more populous than the one that prospered on
the Miami River. A dozen other forts held a more central place than
Fort Dallas did in the Second and Third Seminole Wars. And all six
of Flagler's other hotels in Florida lasted longer, offered more spectacular amenities, and attracted more glamorous guests than did the
Royal Palm Hotel. At times, the North Bank was more mundane than

remarkable. However, the North Bank is more than the sum of its historical parts. It connects the ancient and modern worlds with a series of links that allows us to understand how the Tequesta Indians and other earlier inhabitants of the Miami River built the foundations for the city of Miami long before Julia Tuttle, Henry Flagler, or any of the other city "founders" or so-called pioneers were born.

This volume grapples with the North Bank's enduring history by examining its five eras of human occupation that preceded the 1896 incorporation of the city of Miami. The volume begins with a chapter that discusses the geologic formation of Florida, a reminder that nonhuman forces have helped shape the human history of the site. Environmental historians and archaeologists have long recognized that the natural world and climate change—the altering coastlines, temperatures, and ecosystems—do more than serve as a colorful background for human behavior.

The following five chapters assess how different groups of occupants made the North Bank their home in the centuries that followed the formation of the Miami River. Chapter 2 examines the history of the Tequesta Indians from their arrival some 4,000 years ago until the arrival of the Spanish in 1513. Largely drawn from the archaeological record, this story covers the first and longest-lasting occupation of the region. In this period, the Tequestas proved that history and urban planning occurred even when written records did not. Chapter 3 examines the Tequestas and their experiences under Spanish colonialism. For more than two centuries, the North Bank existed on the edge of the Spanish Empire and as part of the greater Caribbean. This history began with the arrival of Juan Ponce de León and included the subsequent establishment of Spanish missions, a series of slave raids, the effects of repeated shipwrecks, and the influences of Bahamian, Cuban, and other mariners from the region. Chapter 4 explores the various refugees who made the eighteenth-century North Bank their temporary and permanent homes. In this era, hundreds of occupants lived at the North Bank without any adherence to or governance by colonial authorities. Some were enslaved Africans who escaped their bondage, others were Bahamian and Cuban mariners, and some were English banditti under the leadership of William Augustus Bowles. These occupants did not obtain or claim legal possession of the lands, but their presence and de facto ownership of the property was widely acknowledged across the Atlantic. In the nineteenth century, slavery and warfare came to dominate the North Bank. These issues form the core of chapters 5 and 6. The development of chattel slavery at the North Bank reshaped the site's history, especially once the wealthy and influential U.S. citizen Richard Fitzpatrick obtained title over the land in 1830, imported approximately sixty enslaved Africans to the region, and tried to reshape the North Bank to suit the needs of the Atlantic marketplace. The outbreak of war in the 1830s and then again in the 1850s further transformed life at the North Bank. Fitzpatrick abandoned south Florida in 1835, when warfare between U.S. settlers and Seminole Indians engulfed coastal south Florida and the U.S. military repurposed the homestead as a military outpost they called Fort Dallas. When the military occupations ended after the Second and Third Seminole Wars, the North Bank would not remain empty for long. Once again, refugees from across the region—especially after the Civil War began in 1861—occupied the site to escape personal and regional turmoil.

The volume ends where most historians of Miami and south Florida begin, with the arrival of Julia Tuttle and then the construction of the Royal Palm Hotel by Henry Flagler. The epilogue explores how the legendary, and largely self-anointed, pioneers of the late nineteenth and early twentieth centuries built their modern civilization by ignoring and burying the ancient past. With the help of many other pioneers, Tuttle and Flagler fashioned the "infant" city of Miami as a place built from scratch. The opulence of the hotel and the boosterism of its Gilded Age developers obscured its recent and not-so-recent past, allowing historians and others to imagine Florida as largely "untouched by the hand of man." In many ways, the actions of Tuttle and Flagler help explain how prominent scholars could mistakenly proclaim that all of the "successive occupants . . . left such tenuous imprints that by the end of the nineteenth century the area was thought to be as wild and empty as it had been by the sixteenth."[2]

Taken as a whole, I hope that *Before the Pioneers* provides Miami with a sense of its history that has largely been denied. Through little or no fault of their own, Miamians lack a sense of the deep historical terrain that they occupy. It is far too common to hear that Miami is too young to have a distinguished history and that the bulldozer has destroyed all but a few physical reminders of the past. The latter point may be true, as south Florida seems to have an unusually strong devotion to building the modern on the ruins of the old. Many Floridians bemoan the paving of paradise, but few would dare deny that Floridians have routinely erased the old in deference to the new. Demolition and construction have gone hand in hand. Nevertheless, Miami's youth has been greatly overstated, but this view has resulted from a lack of historical awareness rather than a lack of history. The public routinely describes south Florida as a recent creation despite the reality that the human history at the North Bank began before the rise and fall of the Roman Empire and the emergence of Christianity.[3]

Miamians' lack of historical awareness has many causes and reflects a lament that is not unusual in the state. South Floridians from generation to generation discounted the earlier occupants in order to proclaim themselves the rightful occupants of the site. In the process, they have often discarded the importance of their past, described the region as an untouched frontier, and ultimately congratulated themselves for being settlers and pioneers. From ancient times to the present, Miamians have built their civilization on top of the past. The ancient Tequesta Indians—the first residents at the North Bank—literally piled the remains of one generation on top of another, creating the various middens and mounds that proliferate along the coastlines and interior. Fast-forward many hundred years to 1896, when Flagler's construction crews razed a Tequesta burial mound in order to make space for the Royal Palm Hotel. After the hotel opened, the destruction of the past continued. Slave quarters that were later repurposed as officers' quarters for Fort Dallas were moved to nearby Lummis Park during the real estate boom of the early 1920s, and Miami's developers built a new hotel when the hurricane of 1926 destroyed the Royal Palm. As anthropologist Jerald

Milanich explained: "Almost none of the large sites survived the on-slaught of the real estate boom in the 1920s. The same combination of sea and sand that made the region hospitable to American Indians and drew real estate entrepreneurs in the early part of this century continues to draw people to the region."[4]

South Florida may not be unique in this regard, but it certainly has perfected the ability to market the human-made beaches, controlled Everglades, and other "culturally modified landscapes" that schol-ars call "second nature." Other parts hardly feel natural at all. The course of the Miami River has been altered, and the river is now so thoroughly polluted that it is hard to imagine that it was once called "sweet water." Few Miamians, it seems, even know that the river exists or existed. Miami's flora and fauna have been similarly transformed. Nineteenth-century planters tore out mangroves and local fauna and replaced them with imported coconut and guava trees. The coontie plant that sustained the ancient Tequestas and nineteenth-century pioneers still appears in south Florida, but it is primarily found as greenery in cultivated gardens rather than as harvestable wild plants. For its part, the Army Corps of Engineers has dredged and drained so much of the region that most of the physical reminders of the past have been lost. Even Miami's coastline has been transformed as construction crews have straightened and extended the coast into Biscayne Bay. The tropical weather has remained, but concrete and steel block and redirect the natural sea breeze. Non-native plants and animals have crowded out many native species.[5]

The tropical environment has also contributed to the erasure of the physical reminders of the Miami's ancient and not-so-ancient past. The Tequestas as well as the Spanish missionaries built their dwellings out of wood that was efficient and suitable for the region but destined to rot away. Miami's early architecture contrasts sharply with the architecture of the Southwest, where durable adobe bricks lasted and sustained public memories, luring tourists to Taos and the *camino real* that connects the Spanish missions in California. Saltwa-ter, hurricanes, and seasonal rains have obliterated the homes and hotel that once lined the North Bank. Workers would ultimately raze the Royal Palm Hotel, but they did so only after a devastating hurricane in 1926 made it uninhabitable and local officials condemned it.[6]

Miami's lack of historic consciousness also has demographic roots. In recent generations, a combination of migration and immigration, urban sprawl, Everglades drainage, air conditioning, dredging, and various social forces have turned what was once a small town into an international entrepôt. When the twentieth century began, 1,681 people called Miami home, with neighboring Coconut Grove adding an extra 850 people to the population. All of Dade County (which then included the area now considered Broward, Palm Beach, and Monroe Counties) contained fewer than 5,000 residents. A decade later, the city of Miami contained 5,471 people and the county held almost 12,000. The growth has not stopped, although it appeared that it might on a few occasions. By the end of the twentieth century, the city of Miami contained 362,470 residents and more than 2 million people lived in the renamed Miami-Dade County. The tricounty area (which also includes Broward and Palm Beach Counties) now contains more than 5 million people. In a rather short time, Miami was transformed from a small town to the commercial and cultural gateway to and capital of the Caribbean. Biscayne Bay and the North Bank's natural ridge have largely disappeared underneath a stretch of high-rise hotels, condos, parking lots, and office space. Even the natural coastline has disappeared behind acres of artificial lands euphemistically called "fill" that stretch into the bay.[7]

This recent exponential growth aided Miami's historic amnesia. As one scholar quipped for the state as a whole, it contains "so many residents; so few Floridians." Seasonal snowbirds and various other newcomers often learn local (and national) history before coming to recently constructed homes in newly formed Florida housing developments. Not that long ago, one so-called pioneer recalled that at the turn of the twentieth century Miami "was largely a collection of strangers, strangers to the town and to each other. We had all come from somewhere else." This demographic reality still remains true, even as the number of second-generation south Floridians continues to increase. Today only about one in three residents of the state is Florida-born. This lack of sense of place has inevitably shaped how locals understand their history.[8]

Florida's past has also been largely overshadowed as a result of the lengthy Spanish presence in Florida. The United States has generally imagined itself as an extension of English history and otherwise ignored the Native American and Spanish colonial presence. Such oversight into Florida's Native American past is further aided by the lack of a modern Tequesta community that could remind their non-Native neighbors that they lived on ancestral homelands. Furthermore, Floridians too frequently understand the modern Seminoles as migrants rather than as indigenous to the region. By ignoring the connections to ancient Indian communities and centuries of Spanish settlements, many environmental writers simplistically imagine that a "real," natural, and untouched Florida existed only a few generations ago.[9]

Historians and civic boosters have often been no better than Miamians or other writers.[10] Miami's connection to tourism (which largely began with the North Bank's Royal Palm Hotel and continues to serve a central role in the development of the city) created images of sun, beaches, and recreation. It was the "Land of the Sun—The Town That Climate Built." In this version of history, Miami began with Flagler, and Julia Tuttle was the "Mother of Miami." These ideas preclude the idea of a rich and ancient past before tourism. Instead Miami was a "Magic City," which earned the moniker "because of its phenomenal growth on the completion of the East Coast River in 1896." In 1925 local writer Victor Rainbolt typified descriptions of south Florida's history by largely ignoring its ancient or historical roots. He omitted all but a scant mention of the "legend . . . of an extensive [ancient Tequesta] Indian village." Rainbolt, perhaps out of an obligation or to lend romance to his story, included only a brief and misleading discussion of Ponce de León in order to portray the missed opportunities of the past. "Some few centuries ago, Juan Ponce de León discovered the Fountain of Youth in Florida. Had that distinguished gentleman lived in this great day he might have discovered the City of Youth in the same state." Fort Dallas, only because of the enduring legacy of its name, remained a part of the story, even as it overlooked the white settlers, enslaved Africans, and Bahamians who built and occupied it. Similarly, the Seminoles (as either warriors or traders) hardly appear in Rainbolt's narrative. In contrast, he declares that Flagler awoke the site from a "long Rip Van Winkle sleep."[11]

Ironically, the unbroken history at the North Bank is finally getting attention due to the continued resettling of the North Bank. This book—and the HistoryMiami Museum exhibit dedicated to the area—began as a result of the public outcry and contentious mediation that followed the recent archaeological discovery of the site. This discovery remained largely hidden from the public until early 2013, when archaeologist Bob Carr announced that his research team had discovered an unprecedented find in the heart of downtown Miami. Carr unearthed several thousand postholes in the limestone bedrock as well as a treasure trove of other ancient artifacts that date back thousands of years. These artifacts include evidence for the various occupations of the North Bank, including a well that was built by the soldiers at Fort Dallas as well as the front steps to the Royal Palm Hotel. The most notable finds, however, connect the site to the ancient Tequestas. These artifacts include pottery that reveals trade connections to the greater Southeast, axe heads and various tools made from shells and bones, hundreds of shark teeth, and the buried remains of many of the area's ancient inhabitants. Many of the postholes—perhaps the most unique element of the site—form more than a dozen circles on the site, and others seem to connect the circles in straight lines. Although their meaning is still largely unclear, the holes once housed saplings that appear to have formed the foundation for the homes and walkways of the Tequesta Indians who occupied the site thousands of years ago.

This was not the first archaeological discovery related to the Tequesta occupation of south Florida, but the North Bank site dwarfed the earlier discoveries in size and historical importance. It includes what one scholar called the first evidence for urban planning in Florida and what another described as Miami's Garden of Eden. The debate over the territory and its future development took center stage; the developers, preservationists, archaeologists, and various city and county officials all sought to shape the future of the site. Despite their competing ambitions and the posturing by attorneys and others, all of the participants in the debate ultimately agreed that a unique history lay underneath the proposed building on the North Bank of the Miami River. The nature of the limestone underbelly and the sustained development and destruction that had occurred at the location prevented the presence of clear physical strata in the ground. Yet, even with centuries of physical destruction and erasure, the site's history revealed what historian Daniel Richter has described as the "submerged earlier strata" that shape the modern world.[12]

The resulting mediation for the site was an exception to Miami's tendency simply to bury and ignore its past. Instead, the Metropolitan Miami developers of the site redesigned their plans to include an interpretive plaza and to preserve some of the bedrock. Although many preservationists hoped to halt construction or preserve more of the site, the ultimate resolution bridged some of the tensions between historical preservation and urban development. The result largely fulfilled the hopes that archaeologist Bob Carr outlined in his *Digging Miami*, published only a few years before the mediation concluded. "Planners, government regulators, and archaeologists should not see this juggling act between preservation and development as forces in opposition, but as a way for the public good and private property owners to find common ground."[13] The mediation and compromise that resulted in the Met Square development and onsite HistoryMiami Museum will put this somewhat rare optimism to the test.

# Before the North Bank

THE NORTH BANK of the Miami River, like many inhabitants of its shores, is a recent arrival. For most of the earth's history, the bluff or any terrestrial site at this location simply did not exist. The geological and ecological developments that ultimately shaped the North Bank—specifically the formation of Lake Okeechobee, the Everglades, the Miami River, and Biscayne Bay—only occurred around 5,000 years ago. For geologists who work in terrestrial epochs that last hundreds of thousands if not millions of years, the site's lifespan represents a brief moment. The site may be older than our collective memories, but it is not older than dirt.

Unlike the mythical phoenix, Miami and its North Bank emerged out of the water rather than out of the ashes. South Florida existed under a shallow layer of seawater that covered the region and left behind a layer of sandy quartz sediment with layers of limestone and dolestone. Its sandy complexion has been a blessing for phosphate miners but has been the bane of farmers, who for centuries have complained that there is "no true soil on top of it."[1] The Florida peninsula and its beachfront property began to emerge slowly from the waters around 15–20 million years ago, a period that geologists call the Late Oligocene Epoch. Florida's emergence as dry land was temporary, as water would cover large parts of the southern peninsula on at least four different occasions before Florida would reach its current state above sea level. Each of these sustained floods would cover less of the state than the previous one. As a result, the peninsula slowly took shape as the coastlines expanded and contracted in sync with the changing temperatures of the ocean waters. For most of this time Miami's North Bank, or at least its coordinates (25.771364 N 80.188608 W), remained under water.[2]

The last cycle of geologic expansion and contraction ended with an ice age, an epoch when the glaciers swelled and consumed enough of the earth's water to lower the ocean levels by more than 350 feet. This era lasted from about 50,000 to about 13,000 years ago, during which time Florida was much larger. The Atlantic coast extended several miles eastward of its current location and the Gulf coast extended many miles to the west. For most of this period the Florida peninsula was at least twice as large as it is today. The abundant water that defines Miami and the North Bank today had yet to appear. Humidity and standing water (and mosquitos) would eventually arrive, but for thousands of years Miami may have been too dry for human habitation. It existed too far from the Atlantic coast, and fresh water could only be found in isolated sinkholes, natural springs, and sunken pockets in the limestone that covered the Florida peninsula. In these isolated locations, savannahs and dune scrubs formed and sustained the plants and animals that human occupation required. Life could hardly exist elsewhere.[3]

Humans likely arrived in Florida near the end of this ice age and perhaps several millennia before most of Miami become inhabitable. These earliest Floridians probably descended from the Asian migrants who crossed Beringia, a span of land and ice that periodically connected Asia and North America. This "land bridge" existed until around 35,000 years ago, reemerged again from around 22,000 to 17,000 years ago, and then appeared again for the last time from 15,500 to 5,000 years ago. At the end of this period the Bering Strait emerged to separate Alaska from Eastern Asia.[4] Other theories exist to explain the origins of humans in the Americas; some point to ancient Africans, Asians, or Europeans coming to the Americas by water on boats or ice floes. Others proclaim that Native Americans originated in the Americas. Even adherents of the Bering Strait theory debate the timing and nature of humans' crossing and the speed at which the migrants made it to the Florida peninsula. Despite these differences, most of the evidence points to the settling of Florida at least 12,000–14,000 years ago.[5]

Florida may be the farthest point from the Bering Strait in mainland North America, but human beings likely settled in the middle and northern part of the region shortly after the first migrants crossed the land bridge. Some of the best evidence for Florida's antiquity comes from Little Salt Springs, along the Gulf coast of Sarasota County. In this area, archaeologists uncovered some of the oldest artifacts found in the American South, including a 12,000-year-old sharpened stake that was likely used by hunters as well as an ancient deer antler that had been carefully crafted into a measuring tool.[6] At around the same time, ancient Floridians occupied High Springs' Ichetucknee River and created, among other things, a spear point made from mammoth ivory. In addition to confirming the ancient presence of Indians in the territory, the shape of this particular spear point also helps demonstrate the rapid spread of people across North America. Its shape, much to the surprise of many scholars, is similar to the Clovis-style points that hunters used to kill the now extinct Pleistocene animals in New Mexico and elsewhere.[7] The oldest human-made object found in Florida—a fossilized bone with a carved image of a mammoth or mastodon on it—was discovered nearly a century ago in a spring in present-day Vero Beach. The mastodon went extinct at least 13,000 years ago, helping further to establish humans' early presence on the peninsula.[8]

Although these sites have yielded evidence for an ancient presence in Florida, they do not reveal a direct link to a human presence at the North Bank. These artifacts offer only a few glimpses for the Florida's southeastern peninsula in general. Ten thousand years ago, the still-inland site remained rather arid and therefore comparatively uninviting to potential hunters and gatherers elsewhere in the region. Yet humans have lived in the general neighborhood of present-day south Florida for at least about 10,000 years. The best evidence for first

Floridians in the Miami area comes from what is now the Deering Estate at Cutler some 13 miles to the south of the North Bank. The estate was once the bayfront property of Charles Deering—an early twentieth-century art collector whose family's fortune stemmed from the selling of harvesting machines along with their partner, Cyrus McCormick. Thousands of years before Deering established his limestone home and hotel, Native Floridians also visited the site. There, at what is called the Cutler Fossil Site, a solution hole serves as a repository of ancient artifacts. Thousands of years ago, the solution hole collected rain or spring water for much of the year, creating a flourishing "oasis effect" that attracted water-dependent animals to the area. Ancient Floridians frequented these places because they provided reliable sources of water for both themselves and the animals they hunted. As a result, the site contains human and animal remains, a 10,000-year-old spear point, charcoal from an ancient hearth, and evidence that the first Miamians had created various drills, scrapers, and other tools.[9]

We may never know if ancient Floridians visited the landmass that would become known as the North Bank before the waterways that defined it formed. The nature of the archaeological evidence makes it especially unlikely. The Cutler Fossil Site and other archaeological sites in Florida have revealed thousands of pieces of physical evidence that are related to Florida's ancient past. Most commonly, the sites contain spear points that were primarily made from snail and conch shells, shark teeth, and the bones of various animals. These types of physical remains reveal the tendency of Florida's earliest hunters to ambush or attack a wide range of prey near marshes or watering holes and to forage and gather an abundance of wild plants like gourds and hickory nuts. It is also likely that they had some form of political structure to organize hunting expeditions and possibly their daily life. These first Floridians also employed a variety of techniques and materials for making spears, throwing sticks, bolas, adzes, mortars, and other tools. They constructed knives made of shark teeth, pins and needles made of the bones of animals, wooden mortars to grind seeds and nuts, and wooden boomerangs. With their various weapons, they hunted and ate a wide range of animals, including megafauna like mastodons, mammoths, horses, camels, and bison as well as smaller mammals such as deer, rabbits, and raccoons. This lifestyle allowed these migratory Floridians to be more stable and semisedentary than modern-day images of big-game hunters would often lead people to believe.[10]

Around 9,500 years ago, around the same time as the oldest evidence at Miami's Cutler Fossil Site, the earth began to warm. These climatic changes had a profound effect on the Florida peninsula and its inhabitants. Rising temperatures ushered in a series of transformations that ultimately made the North Bank the center of human behavior in the region. For starters, the warming climate made Florida's land mass smaller and wetter, as the Atlantic coastline hesitatingly began to move toward its present-day location. The physical North Bank and its geographic surroundings would not exist for several thousand more years, but during the early Archaic period the Atlantic coast slowly ceded ground to a strait of water that would later become Biscayne Bay. Indeed, most of the modern watering holes, creeks, lakes, wetlands, mangroves, beaches, barrier islands, and coasts did not form until thousands of years later. During this era, south Florida also became part of the subtropics—with an ecosystem accustomed to the heat, humidity, and ocean breezes. The rising temperatures further coincided with a wave of extinctions that erased Florida's population of mastodons, mammoths, giant sloths, camels, llamas, horses, and saber-toothed cats.[11]

During the Archaic period, Florida's human populations underwent tremendous changes while adjusting to the wetting of south Florida and the extinctions of the animals that they depended upon for survival. Although no evidence suggests that Indians occupied the North Bank during this period, the Cutler Fossil Site and others point to presence of Native Floridians in the southern part of the peninsula. The Indians of the southern interior migrated away from the disappearing shores and closer to the new coastlines and to the interior. They may have also moved north to take advantage of the wetter climates there. These Indians replaced the large spear points designed for hunting the now extinct megafauna with smaller and lighter weapons. Those who settled along the coasts relied on nets (cordage) to catch sea animals, and the archaeological record reveals their persistent reliance on shellfish and other marine life for sustenance.[12]

Perhaps the best, and certainly most unique, Archaic evidence on the Florida peninsula is found at the Windover Archaeological Site near Titusville on the Atlantic coast. There, in a peat-bottomed bog, archaeologists have unearthed an ancient cemetery with at least 168 skeletons, many of which still contain brain matter. When discovered, the bodies were uncharacteristically well preserved because of the nearly neutral pH level of the watery grave as well as the anaerobic atmosphere created by the peat that covered the bodies. The human remains date to between 7,330 and 8,120 years old, and the survival of the brain matter demonstrates the community's commitment to burying the deceased within 48 hours. Other evidence comes from the presence of grave goods that include textile wraps, antler-bone awls, shark teeth, and stone projectile points. The pond also contains baskets, twine, and other materials rarely found in the Archaic archaeological record. Their preservation illuminates the roots of the ancient cultures that would ultimately establish themselves a few hundred miles to the south at the North Bank.[13]

The people of Windover, like the Tequestas at the North Bank, formed a largely sedentary community who survived by a combination of hunting, fishing, and gathering. They likely lived in the nut- and berry-rich area in the spring and summer and perhaps wintered along the banks of the nearby Indian River. They feasted on snails and mussels from local waterways, designed prestige items like jewelry and toys, devised various tools from wood and bones, and created at least seven different textile patterns woven from palm fronds. Some of these textiles required the use of looms—another technical innovation of the era. Although some of the bodies show signs of distress and trauma, other graves revealed that the ancient Floridians had tremendous concern for the sick. The gravesite, for example, includes one woman with a belly full of what seems to be a medicine made of berries and roots, a 50-year-old woman who had lived several years after suffering from debilitating bone fractures, and a young teenager who died after battling the symptoms of spina bifida for most if not all of his life. The latter two seemed to die of natural causes, pointing to a community that was willing to care for rather than abandon those who required assistance for their daily needs.[14]

Windover and other Archaic sites in Florida point to a divergence in the ancient world, a split that in many ways separated the experiences of coastal and southern Florida from the rest of the American South. Whereas many of the interior groups in North America began experimenting with food cultivation and ultimately corn agriculture, the Indians in south Florida pursued different ecological opportunities. These opportunistic hunters relied on a wide range of locally available animals, nuts, and plants for their survival. The ecosystem (and climate) of south Florida provided more than sufficient resources to its inhabitants. Native Floridians did not have to move very far, if at all, to avail themselves of the bounties of the various seasons. They could meet their basic and often not-so-basic needs within rather close proximity. Perhaps most important, the presence of water allowed south Florida Indians to fish with nets and collect shellfish rather efficiently.[15]

As the region became wetter, Florida's Indians increasingly relied on dugout canoes to crisscross their way across the peninsula. This mode of transportation allowed the Indians to exploit the interior as well as the coastline of Florida and helped facilitate trade and diplomacy with more distant groups. The use of canoes allowed people to cross the gulf, created trade routes to Caribbean islands, and otherwise fostered long-distance trade and travel. Florida's Indians also used the canoes to travel to their temporary camps in their search for specific game and raw materials. As a result, the permanent communities that they established across the southern part of the Florida peninsula—places often called base camps—came to display a greater diversity of material goods.[16]

The topography and climate of south Florida would take its contemporary shape around 3,200–5,500 years ago. Although ecological and climatic oscillations continued, south Florida's environment approached what it is today. The sea level at the time settled just around four feet lower than modern levels, which led to the contracting of the coasts and the flooding of the many inland depressions in the Florida peninsula. In south Florida, this changing water table allowed the Big Cypress Swamp and the Everglades to become significantly wetter than they had been. Hammocks formed in Florida's interior with mangroves along the coast. These tidal forests take their name from *mangue* (the Portuguese word for tree and grove—the English word for a group of trees) and otherwise reveal the meeting of cultures that would ultimately occur on the Miami shores.[17]

By the end of this era, the North Bank of the Miami River had formed at what could be considered the "rim of the Everglades." Biscayne Bay transformed from a narrow sea channel to a flooded outlet on the southeastern Atlantic coast. Water levels continued to rise but stabilized at about one inch every 100 years, allowing the region to appear fixed. The mangroves along the shoreline and the coral reefs just offshore emerged as vibrant ecosystems, attracting various life forms that came to define south Florida's natural history. The Everglades, which had been slowly taking shape, stabilized as a unique ecosystem that dumped some of its waters into the Atlantic through the Miami River.[18] Over time, as the river's waters cut deeper into the peninsula, a small ridge on the coast emerged. Mangroves and the flow of tides made a permeable boundary between the land and sea, but a Tequesta Indian community slowly made the ridge its home.

As the Miami River took shape, Native peoples traversed the new travel route and began the North Bank's human history. Until recently, most scholars dated the human history of the site to 2,000 years ago. The analysis of ceramics and other artifacts recently uncovered from the site and elsewhere in the southeastern part of the United States points to a much earlier use for the site. Scholars now believe that late Archaic Indians—who would become known as the Tequestas—occupied the site as long as 3,500–4,000 years ago. These Tequesta visitors likely came through the Miami River and Biscayne Bay as they participated in a regional trade network that connected the community at Fort Center near Lake Okeechobee with the Calusas on Florida's west coast, the Mississippian peoples in north Florida, Georgia, and beyond, and various Indian communities in the Caribbean. Scholars—in large part due to the data unearthed at the North Bank in the early twenty-first century—will undoubtedly continue to transform our understanding of Tequesta culture and the arrival of these people in the area of the Miami River.[19]

# THE FOUNDERS

AROUND 2,000 YEARS AGO, the ancestors of the Tequesta Indians set up a permanent settlement along the Miami River and began a history of permanent human occupation that continues to shape modern Miami. Scholars will likely never know what the Indians on the Miami River called themselves in this period, but they laid the foundation for the community that the Spanish would ultimately know as the Tequestas. In establishing the North Bank's first sedentary community, the Tequestas added a human element to the transformation of the local environment. Their ancestors left their mark on south Florida as a whole, but effects of their ancestor's behavior were largely dwarfed by the results of naturally occurring climate change. The ancient Tequestas were different. The natural world did not disappear on their watch, but it increasingly reflected the ambitions and intentions of its human occupants. The Tequestas hunted land animals and harvested sea life to a degree that often exhausted local populations. They also helped desirable plants spread along the coast and built structures that were designed to last more than the season. Mother nature, of course, continued to shape Tequesta lives as they struggled with winds, tides, storms, and floods. Unwanted plants retained an uncanny ability to crowd out desirable ones, and the migrations of animals brought uncertainty to the food supply. Nonetheless, the Tequestas thrived by extracting a surplus of resources from the natural environment of the North Bank. With their particular ecological opportunities and limitations, the Tequestas culturally modified the environment to transform it into what is known as "second nature."[1]

The Indians at the North Bank were part of a larger community that archaeologists call the Granada Site, which includes several middens and mounds that have long since been destroyed on both the north side and south side of the river. Shortly after Granada first attracted scientific interest in 1879, the lasting monuments of the Tequesta site underwent a systemic destruction and intensive development that continues to the present. In the late nineteenth century, construction workers cleared the mounds and destroyed much of the evidence on the lost world of the Tequestas. Rocks, sands, and various building materials were added to create new foundations, middens were leveled and their contents spread across the terrain, and skulls were reburied with disdain. The process mixed Mississippian era trade goods, Glades era ceramics, and shark teeth and vertebrae likely from the early historic Tequestas with Spanish olive jars and glass shards from more recent years. As a result, according to one scholar, "Just about any conclusion about the east coast must be carefully qualified," because "the Tequesta are at once among the best and the least known of the south Florida peoples."[2]

We will likely never know exactly when or why the Tequesta Indians chose to occupy the North Bank around 2,000 years ago. The Tequestas established several other communities in south Florida before they established a permanent settlement at the mouth of the Miami River. In what is now the south Broward County community of Weston, the presence of 5,000-year-old bones points to the possible presence of the Tequestas even before the Miami River formed. More recent sites demonstrate the early existence of the Tequestas with significantly more certainty. Madden's Hammock, in what is now Miami Lakes, served as a burial site some 2,500 years ago. Other sites in south Florida point to the wider presence and older history of the Tequestas beyond the area along Biscayne Bay. These Indians most likely came down the Miami River or through Biscayne Bay as part of a regional trade network that passed ceramics, precious spiritual items, and other trade goods across the region.

This community would ultimately become the cultural and demographic epicenter of the Tequesta polity, with as many as 1,000 of the approximately 10,000 Tequestas living at or near the mouth of the Miami River. The community likely extended out from the North Bank, with much of the potential evidence for the settlement hidden below the foundations of modern Miami. Excavation at the North Bank, however, revealed the presence of thousands of round holes in the limestone underbelly, pointing to the likelihood that the Tequestas built a few dozen round buildings and potentially raised walkways to connect them. Many more holes may still remain hidden underneath the surrounding buildings and roads. It is unclear whether any (or how many) of the discovered homes coexisted with one another or whether the buildings were rebuilt years apart from one another. Archaeologists at the North Bank site also unearthed the strewn remains of middens and mounds, pointing to the locale's connection to other major Native peoples in the southeast and Caribbean. These findings include pottery shards from Mississippian peoples in Georgia and north Florida as well as hundreds of various tools made from the shells, bones, and teeth of the animals that were prevalent in south Florida.[3]

It is not hard to imagine why the Tequestas would ultimately find the North Bank location so desirable. At the time, Miami was significantly wetter than today's Miami because it lacked the systematic drainage programs of the past century. Before the modern apparatus of "water control," the Everglades was an endless wetland, a sheet of south-flowing waters that extended unevenly from Lake Okeechobee to the southern tip of the peninsula. Waters from five headwaters flowed into the lake, and seasonal flooding allowed the wetlands to define the entirety of the southern peninsula. In this environment where seasonal rains averaged around 60 inches per year, the Tequestas put a premium on lands that were a few feet above sea level. The mangroves and islands of the Everglades provided permanent and temporary relief from the flowing and rising waters. The Atlantic

Coastal Ridge—a stretch of limestone along the eastern coast that was five to twenty-five miles in length—offered similar security. Most Tequesta communities formed at the mouths of various waterways or along the coasts. The North Bank provided all of these favorable ecological conditions. In the era leading up to its occupation, the sea level changed a few feet, bringing the shoreline up to the modern location of the bluff. If dry land was "prime real estate," a bluff safely above sea level with easy access to the river and bay must have been seen as a blessing for a people reliant on water and trade routes for their survival. Once the Tequestas established their community on the North Bank, it remained the centerpiece of their life until European colonialism led to its destruction in the seventeenth century.[4]

The North Bank had other distinctions that the Tequestas and later occupants found valuable. One of these advantages was the prevalence of coontic plants (*Zamia floridana*). This cycad with light green leathery leaves and a large root has historically been an important part of Miami's history. The poisonous root of the coontie plant can be pounded or ground and then repeatedly soaked and strained to yield an edible flour that became a mainstay of the Tequesta diet. When processed incorrectly, the flour contained enough cycasin to be fatal; when prepared properly, however, the toxin washes away and the flour can be used to thicken stews or kneaded (when mixed with water) into a slightly sweet bread. It is unclear whether the Tequestas created the process to create coontie flour or learned it from one of their many neighbors, as Native peoples throughout Florida, the Caribbean, and Latin America similarly created starches from various species of *Zamia*. In any case, they certainly relied on it. The location of the North Bank of the Miami River provided easy access to the coontie plant as well as to the waterways that enabled the Tequestas to turn coontie flour into an important trade good in their dealings with their inland Native American neighbors. The coontie flour is naturally resistant to spoilage and therefore has been used to make biscuits and wafers for travelers. In addition, the leftover pulp became an effective fertilizer and food for animals. After years of captivity in Florida, the Spaniard Hernando d'Escalante Fontaneda recalled that they "make bread of roots, which is their common food the greater part of the time." In this way, the starchy flour provided a consistent form of sustenance except for when "the roots cannot be reached" on account of floodwaters. These floods hardly affected the people on the North Bank who could harvest the plants along the ridge and coastal ridge all year. The Tequestas created this starch with a technology that would be replicated by others in the Miami area until the twentieth century.[5]

By the time the Tequestas occupied the North Bank, they had already undergone significant cultural changes and otherwise adapted to the environment of south Florida. This process of ecological adaption created one of the regional variants of Indian culture that some scholars have termed the Glades culture—a term that reflects their proximity and reliance on the Everglades. The Glades culture extended up and down the eastern coast of south Florida and into the interior, an area that encompasses much of modern Miami-Dade, Broward, Palm Beach, Monroe, and Hendry Counties. The influence of the Glades culture was felt most along the coast, although the Tequestas also occupied the high ground mangroves of the Everglades. Most experts accept the idea that three major geographic variations of Glades culture likely existed as distinct cultural and political units. The Calusas lived along the western gulf; the Jaegas thrived to the north in what is now Palm Beach and Martin Counties; and the Tequestas lived along the Atlantic and various bays to the south. Other Native Americans (sometimes distinguished as distinctive cultures or lumped with the three coastal groups) occupied the interior surrounding Lake Okeechobee. The Tequestas may have stretched from as far south as the Keys and as far north as modern-day Boca Raton, although most scholars believe that they lived in a significantly smaller area focused around the ceremonial center of the North End of the Miami River and the Biscayne Bay area more generally.[6]

The Tequestas' permanent occupation of the North Bank began during what scholars call the Glades I period (2,500 to 1,250 years ago). Over the next 1,500 years, the Tequesta society continuously changed as they employed new pottery techniques and motifs, erected large mound structures and ceremonial centers, embraced new food taboos, and incorporated cultural influences from the north and elsewhere. These changes—which scholars use to distinguish the emergence of subsequent historical eras called Glades II and Glades III—accompanied demographic growth as well as modifications in social and political stratification. With some regional differences, all of the people of the Glades survived "on the exploitation of the food resources of the tropical coastal waters, with secondary dependence on game and some use of wild food plants." The differences between the eras are important not just for the sake of historic accuracy but also as a reminder that even traditional peoples experimented and innovated in ways that are often lost in the retelling of their histories.[7]

During this historical transformation, the Tequestas along the North Bank developed a way of life that took advantage of their location on the river and bay as well as their place along a coastal ridge on the edge of the wetlands. Unlike most Indians of the Southeast and northern Florida, the Tequestas were not agriculturalists. Whereas most of the southeastern Indians relied on the three sisters—maize, beans, and squash—as a nutritional and economic foundation, the Tequestas established a mound-building and hierarchical community without these staples. Early Europeans as well as earlier generations of archaeologists tended to see the lack of maize and horticulture in Tequesta society as evidence for their lack of sophistication, but the Tequestas and other south Florida Indians defied these norms. Despite theories that see agriculture as a necessary precondition for social complexity, Tequesta society demonstrates that this was not the case. The Tequestas lived in a hierarchical society, with a main chief extracting obedience and gifts from surrounding village leaders. The brother of the chief, it seems, also had the ability to speak for the chief. In addition, the Tequestas had leading men and other leaders who were not necessarily related to the chief.[8]

A lack of agriculture did not mean a lack of food. In addition to harvesting and processing coontie, the Tequestas extracted a bounty of natural resources from the Everglades, the Miami River, and Biscayne Bay. The estuary (the area where river waters entered the bay) was remarkably productive, and the mangrove forests contained many species of fish and other sea animals. In addition, some Tequesta men (and perhaps women and families too) likely left the permanent settlement at the North Bank to travel to temporary campsites inland and to neighboring islands and sandbars in search of additional resources. At these special-use camps, the Tequestas fished, gathered seafood, hunted, harvested coontie, and performed other specialized tasks. Some scholars believe that they were a coastal people in the fall and winter, moving into the interior during the summer. Both there and on the coast, they hunted, trapped, and ate manatee, sharks, sailfish, porpoises, stingrays, swordfish, oysters, conch, and countless other species of fish and shellfish. Their diet also relied on a wide range of land animals. They hunted deer, turtles, and various other small animals nearby. They also gathered wild subtropical fruits such as sea grapes, huckleberries, pigeon plums, wild figs, prickly pears, and palmetto berries. They ate many of these foods fresh but also dried the berries and meats for use while traveling and to protect against shortages. The Tequestas used various technologies to gather food, including fiber nets, weirs, net floats made of gourds, and tidal traps. They made knives from shark teeth; knives and scrapers from shells and stone; barbs and points from sailfish beaks and stingray tails; bone projectile points; and harpoons and fishhooks from various other resources. As expert wood carvers, they created utilitarian as well as ceremonial items from the natural world around them. They were resourceful and not hungry.[9]

The Tequesta community at the mouth of the Miami straddled the river. On the south bank, the Tequestas constructed a settlement most known for what was likely a ceremonial center (site 8DA1212). Commonly referred to today as the Miami Circle or the Brickell Point Site, the site was discovered in 1998 during the downtown construction of condominiums. It consists of twenty-four holes of various shapes that the Tequestas cut into the limestone bedrock around the same time that they occupied the North Bank. These holes, along with hundreds of additional smaller holes, form a nearly perfect 38-foot circle that likely supported the walls of a ceremonial structure.

Scholars continue to debate the purpose and design of the formation, but one of the most convincing theories holds that the Tequestas congregated at the site for ceremonial purposes or that it may have housed the community's spiritual leader. Others have suggested that it was the base of an astronomic site akin to Stonehenge (or Woodhenge at Cahokia in Illinois). Some modern Indians, most vocally Bobby C. Billie of the Independent Traditional Seminole Nation, have proclaimed it to be sacred. The circular building on the site likely mirrored the cone-shaped thatched structures that were used across the river and elsewhere in North America. These buildings typically had a hole in the thatching to allow smoke to escape and were framed with bent tree saplings. These theories on the Miami Circle are supported by the presence of ceremonial items made from pumice at the site and by the presence of unused stone (basalt) axes made from raw materials from the Appalachian Mountains. These ceremonial items point to the potential sacred nature of the site.[10] The origins of the Miami Circle will continue to be debated, but many experts agree that it was "an early component of a major Native American village" that straddled the Miami River.[11]

The recently discovered North Bank community shared characteristics with other centralized Tequesta villages. The Tequestas established most of their villages at the mouths of rivers or coastal lagoons and lived in these villages most if not all of the year. This settlement pattern ensured ample space for hunting and fishing between the sites. The North Bank also contained the two differently shaped buildings that typified Tequesta architectures. As at other Tequesta sites, one style approximated the longhouses along the eastern coast of the United States, while the other style consisted of small circular homes built of bent saplings and covered thatched roofs. These buildings were likely made of palm fronds, straw, and wood, which required constant replacement and have long decomposed. As a result, the archaeological record tells us only a little about the Tequestas' buildings. The written record from after the arrival of the Spaniards reveals little more. Most descriptions amount to little more than a few words about the presence of Tequesta "huts" or of the presence

Figure 1. The North Bank of the Miami River became the site of intensive archaeological research during the construction of the Met Square complex in 2014. Led by Robert Carr, archaeologists unearthed a wealth of information. For example, they delineated the location of the ancient mangroves and natural waterline on the upper right. Photograph courtesy of Lisa Tendrich Frank, 2014.

of the "house of the cacique [leader]."[12] Perhaps because of the seemingly rugged and seasonal nature of their buildings, Gabriel Díaz Vara Calderón overlooked the durability of the homes and concluded that the Tequestas "had no fixed abodes."[13] Nevertheless, it is likely that the Tequestas had palmetto-thatched roofs like those later used by the Seminoles in the region and Native peoples throughout the Caribbean.[14]

In addition, the Tequestas also built several mounds on or near the site, at least one of which was a burial mound. The mounds were ultimately razed in the late nineteenth century, as construction workers found them to be a nuisance in the building of the Royal Palm Hotel. One of the men leveling the site declared that "it stood out like a small mountain, twenty to twenty-five feet above water" and "about one hundred feet long and seventy feet wide." Other raised shell middens were still visible in the early twentieth century before they too were razed and flattened in the name of development. Different mounds served varied purposes, and their destruction in the modern era has limited the ability to assess their original functions. In certain Tequesta and coastal communities in Florida, religious and political leaders lived on the tops of some mounds. Other shell mounds (or middens) were frequently part of permanent villages but also next to fishing or oyster-gathering camps. These ancient garbage dumps grew as generations of settlers discarded pottery, oyster shells, and other organic materials into nearby piles. Without knowing their exact purpose, archaeologists consider the remains of these mounds to be evidence of early inhabitants.[15]

The Tequestas' main form of transportation made the North Bank ideal. In the ancient and historic eras, the Indians in Florida routinely traveled by dugout canoes and cut paths through the sawgrass and other foliage of the Everglades. By carving (and scraping) these seaworthy canoes from trees, the Tequestas ventured into the bay, obtained reliable access to many of the Caribbean islands, and made connections with the Native communities along the Gulf and Atlantic coasts. Dugout canoes came in many sizes, and large ones could typically carry a dozen passengers and some cargo. The Tequestas also used their canoes to travel up the Miami River to their temporary camps, hunt animals in the interior, harvest the nuts and fruits of palm and other trees, and gather coontie from interior lands.[16]

The unpredictability of rain and the uneven topography of the Everglades required the Tequestas and other Indians of the Glades to cut paths through the sawgrass and build long-distance canals to make these paths more permanent. Some paths existed naturally, as the flow of water inhibited the growth of plants in narrow but long stretches of the Everglades. Constant use further widened the paths, creating what amounted to a network of constructed and natural waterways that connected various villages with one another. As a result, the Tequestas and other Glades Indians reshaped the mangrove islands and the Everglades more generally to foster travel and trade.[17]

The omnipresence of rain made watercraft an essential part of Tequesta diplomacy and trade. The Tequestas forged trading and diplomatic alliances with the Ais to the north and the Calusas to the west as well as the Indians in the interior. The relationship between the Calusas and Tequestas, which is documented by a scattered evidentiary record, changed over time. Most academic interpretations agree that the Tequestas were connected politically rather than culturally to the powerful Calusas and that these connections were temporary rather than permanent. The two groups spoke different languages, had different pottery technologies and motifs, and otherwise seem to have sustained only limited contact with one another. Some scholars believe that the Calusas came to dominate the Tequestas around 1100, with the cacique (chief) of the Calusas expecting obedience from the cacique of the Tequestas. Archaeologist John Mann Goggin, for example, described the Calusas as dominant "overlords" whom the Tequestas and others occasionally disobeyed. More recently, historian John H. Hann has explained that Tequestas were (at least at times) a tributary to Chief Carlos, of the Calusa. These diplomatic relationships, like those among many peoples at the time, likely resulted from a policy of arranged marriages between ruling families. In this manner, blood relationships helped cement ties between the communities. Despite their linguistic barriers, the Tequestas and Calusas had many connections.[18]

The complexity of Tequesta society extended beyond their diplomatic and economic connections to their neighbors. Although analysis of the data from the North Bank is still in its infancy, other Glades sites have provided remarkable insight into the ancient Tequestas and their neighbors. The ancient Indians of south Florida created intricately carved and painted wooden masks, wooden plaques, toy boats, and ceremonial canoe paddles. In Marco Island, for example, Frank Hamilton Cushing uncovered two effigy masks (the heads of a wolf and an alligator) with movable parts.[19] Some glimpses of the Tequesta's spiritual world and culture emerge though these items. Written accounts from the earliest Spanish observers add to these details. Some accounts proclaim that in Tequesta society "the sun was worshipped under the semblance of a stuffed deer."[20] There are also reports, albeit from unreliable sources, that the Tequesta Indians engaged in human sacrifice. Not surprisingly, these accounts tend to follow tropes for non-Christian peoples in both fictional and firsthand accounts.[21] More reliable accounts, though, point to symbolic acts of cannibalism. James Adair, a white trader who married into the Cherokee nation before writing a history of the region, wrote that the Creeks who captured many Tequestas declared that they were not cannibals per se. Although noting "the least inclination they ever had of eating human flesh," Adair did relate that the Tequestas ate "only the heart of the enemy, which they all do, symbolically (blood for blood) in order to inspire them with courage; yet the constant losses they suffered might have highly provoked them to exceed their natural barbarity."[22] Such language reflected Adair's desire to emphasize the "savagery" of ancient Indian culture.

Some of the most interesting and revealing details about Tequesta society relate to their complicated burial practices. Several accounts point to the reverence that the Tequestas showed for the bones of loved ones and leaders. According to one written account, the death of a chief resulted in a solemn series of rituals. Upon the death of a "leading man," the community or select members of the community "take him apart" and sort the large bones from the rest. "They bury the little bones with the body"; then "in the cacique's house they place a large box and they enclose the large bones in this box and the whole village comes there to adore and they hold these bones as their gods." The box remains in the house until the winter, when the community sends "all the canoes . . . out to the sea" in search of a manatee. When they find one, a selected Indian kills it in order to "extract two bones that it has in the skull" and puts them "in this chest in which they place the deceased."[23] Another account states that after the deceased is "stripped and dismembered . . . the bones are carefully cleaned and distributed among the kinsmen and friends, the largest bones going to the nearest and dearest. Then a bonfire is made and the flesh is thrown into the flames, while around the fire a mournful chant and dance goes on."[24]

The Tequestas' style of clothing, it seems, was largely a function of the available resources, but they may have been more complex than our stereotypical images of ancient Indians. Several written accounts describe the Tequestas as covering their bodies with Spanish moss, woven palmetto, and tanned animal skins. It is also likely that they wore "breech-clouts of plaited straw." This seemed to be the case for Ais and Calusas, the Tequestas' trading and diplomatic partners to the north and west. The use of woven fibers in their clothes is also probable, because weaving techniques predate the Tequestas' arrival in south Florida and their construction of various fishing nets from similar raw materials. The Tequestas also likely adorned their bodies with tattoos and other forms of body art. Techniques for creating these tattoos differed across Native North America, but most cultures used needles or sharpened points crafted from various animals or plants and then rubbed natural dyes into the skin to create the desired design. It is unclear how the Tequestas tattooed themselves, but Seminoles and other Indians relied on everything from pine needles to sharpened bones and used octopus ink, ash, and other dyes.[25]

Before the 1513 arrival of Juan Ponce de León, Native Americans had lived in a permanent village at the mouth of the Miami River for roughly 1,500 years. With a village on one side and a ceremonial center on the other, at least 1,000 residents made the location their home. The Spanish called this village "Tequesta" (in various spellings) and agreed that the site was the heart of a unique Indian community. In the century that followed, the swirling forces of colonialism would transform the Tequestas' world. As Christian missionaries, slave raiders, traders, and others sought to incorporate the Tequestas into the expanding Atlantic world, the Indians themselves would suffer and ultimately lose their ancient foothold in Miami.

# Spanish Colonialism and the Doctrine of Discovery

On July 3, 1513, less than three months after his initial "discovery" of Florida, Juan Ponce de León sailed into Biscayne Bay. León had briefly passed through the bay a couple of months earlier, but this time his crew lingered long enough for him to become familiar with the coastal geography and the people who lived there. It is unclear whether León stepped ashore, but his crew provided the first written record of the North Bank and its "Chequeschá" or "Jequesta" residents. Even so, the discovery did not even merit a sentence in the official annals. Antonio Herrera y Tordesilla, the state-sanctioned historian of León's journey, declared that they "reached Chequeschá" before wrapping up the entire 1513 mission in a few pages.[1]

León visited the North Bank as part of a larger journey designed to "get information," "take possession," and "increase his estate." After initially landing to the northeast on the Atlantic coast (likely near present-day Cape Canaveral), his armada of three armed vessels sailed around the tip of Florida to the Gulf coast near Charlotte Harbor. León's crew spent nine days in the area, fighting with the local Calusa Indians and angering their chief, Carlos. León's crew of about sixty-five men did more than wage war. They also traded with the Calusas, secured water and firewood, and searched for gold to enrich the Spanish Empire. León got unexpected assistance from a Spaniard who had lived among the Calusas since his capture during an earlier Spanish raid. The captive served as an interpreter, but he hardly kept the peace. León and the Spanish invaders took at least four captives before they were chased out of west Florida. As they fled, the conquistadors traveled through the Keys and up Florida's Atlantic coast into Biscayne Bay.[2]

León did not discover Florida or the North Bank. Such a statement would discount the presence of its earlier occupants, the Paleoindians who first occupied the region and the Tequestas, Calusas, Apalachees, Timucuas, and other Indian communities who lived in Florida when León arrived. From the perspective of the Spanish Crown, however, Native peoples lacked what the Europeans considered proper jurisdiction over their ancestral lands. Under the doctrine of discovery, León and others disregarded governments that existed outside of the recognized monarchical governments of western Europe. According to León, Indians held the right to occupancy, but tribal peoples lacked sovereignty or property rights. As much as the Spanish routinely turned Indian leaders into "kings" and "princesses," they claimed that only Christian nations possessed legitimate ownership.[3]

The doctrine of discovery helps explain why León receives credit for discovering Florida (and the North Bank) when he was not the first European to visit Florida's shores. Other Spaniards visited the peninsula before 1513 in the pursuit of Indian slaves, fish, water, lumber, and other commodities. With Cuba only 90 miles to the south and fewer than 200 miles separating the Bahamas from the Florida coast, enterprising European sailors visited Florida and returned home with unconfirmed reports of it being an island, a geological misperception that persisted for years. In 1511 these rumors reached Spain. The Crown granted León a royal contract to explore the "islands of Bimini" and the region north of Cuba. This charter turned unconfirmed speculation into state-sanctioned facts. During his 1513 mission, León learned much that the Crown did not know. His discoveries included the North Bank of the Miami River, Biscayne Bay, and its Tequesta inhabitants. If León *discovered* Florida, it was only because he was the first man that a Christian government sanctioned to do so.[4]

※

The arrival of the Spanish had an immeasurable impact on the North Bank and its Tequesta inhabitants. Disease, slave raids, trade, settlements, warfare, missionaries, and the other forces of colonialism transformed and destabilized Native American communities in countless ways. Europeans introduced new plants and animals to the continent, and the environmental distinctions between Europe and the Americas slowly became less obvious when citrus fruits, sugarcane, and cattle became part of Florida's natural world. This "Columbian Exchange" ultimately had a devastating effect on American Indians, as newly introduced pathogens spread smallpox, influenza, and other diseases in unprecedented epidemics. Native communities struggled to survive the turmoil. Even so, the Tequestas' old world did not instantly shatter in 1513 to be replaced by a new landscape. For more than two centuries after León's discovery, the North Bank remained a centerpiece of a unique Tequesta society.[5]

At first Europeans deemed the North Bank to be a risky if not worthless locale. Spaniards called it a "low, sterile land" that was "deserted and of little benefit." The French, who would briefly challenge Spain's control of Florida, agreed. René Goulaine de Laudonnière, who founded French Fort Caroline in northeastern Florida in 1564, declared that "the tip of Florida was a marshy area and therefore unsuitable for our habitation, as it was a place which would bring neither profit to the King nor contentment or pleasure to use if we inhabited the land." With few exceptions, most Europeans who visited the region in the sixteenth century shared Laudonnière's view. Even Spanish governor Pedro Menéndez, who visited and sanctioned the creation of a mission on the site, explained that "it is very poor land, subject to inundation, and the Indians cannot sustain themselves except on roots and shellfish."[6]

The Tequestas' lack of agriculture made the North Bank particularly unsuitable for Spain's colonial ambitions. Spain built its

American empire by extracting tribute, labor, and precious metals from Native peoples. Spain wanted to administer an expansive and extractive operation by creating "republics of Indians" where Native people performed most of the administrative and physical labor. This process worked especially well in hierarchical Mesoamerica, where Spanish officials brutally destabilized the Mayas and Aztecs and obtained alliances with leaders who could extract the desired resources. The Spanish Crown, perhaps overoptimistically, had similar hopes for the conquest of the corn-growing Apalachees and Timucuas in north Florida. They had even less ambition for their prospects at the North Bank. A lack of precious gold and silver—what Fontaneda called "no product of mines"—limited the region's desirability. Just as important, Spanish hopes were limited by the Tequestas' lack of agriculture, significantly smaller population, and territory, which they deemed (rather naively) to be an ecological desert.[7]

Despite these perceived shortcomings, the North Bank eventually became an important part of the Spanish Empire. It did so largely because of its proximity to Havana, a city declared to be the "Key to the New World and Bulwark of the West Indies." The North Bank was just 230 miles away from the commercial and diplomatic entrepôt, located along the thoroughfare that connected Havana with Seville and many of Spain's colonial interests along North America's Atlantic coast. The North Bank was rarely a planned destination, but many boats in the sixteenth century came to the vicinity as a result of tropical storms, poorly charted waters, the "uncooperativeness of the winds," and the need to obtain fresh water, lumber, and other supplies. These sailors provided most of the earliest information about the North Bank and the Tequestas. Hernando d'Escalante Fontaneda, a shipwrecked Spaniard who spent seventeen years among the Calusa Indians, left the most detailed description. For many years, sailors knew little more than what Fontaneda wrote in 1549: "the Indians called Tequesta [are] situated on the bank of a river which extends into the country the distance of fifteen leagues, and issues from another lake of fresh water, which is said by some Indians . . . to be an arm of the Lake of Mayaimi [Lake Okechobee]."[8]

In 1565 one of these unintended journeys integrated the North Bank and its Tequesta residents into the Spanish Empire. On its journey north to help establish the permanent settlement of St. Augustine, one of Governor Pedro Menéndez's ships anchored in Biscayne Bay to escape a particularly fierce storm. As the crew waited out the rough weather, the Spaniards traded with the Tequestas and made a brief but important diplomatic contact. Unbeknownst to Menéndez, the Spanish governor and the Tequesta leader were already connected diplomatically because of preexisting relationships in Native Florida. These connections shaped Menéndez's reception by the Indians at the North Bank. Once it became known that the Spanish leader had once ransomed his young daughter from the Calusas when she was about "nine or ten years of age," the Tequesta chief (named Tequesta) bestowed food and gifts on Menéndez. The Tequestas' embrace of Menéndez increased when the Indians learned of his marriage to the sister of the now-allied Calusa chief.[9]

A year later, one hundred mutineers accidentally reinforced Menéndez's earlier contact. After abandoning their posts in San Mateo (Fort Carolina) in north Florida, they anchored near the North Bank as they fled toward Havana. A storm pushed their anchored ship out to sea and marooned twenty of the men who had gone ashore. Soon after, "a contrary wind" sent Pedro Menéndez Márquez ashore as he investigated rumors of a French settlement in south Florida. Márquez, the governor's cousin, discovered that the Tequestas had saved the mutineers. The Spaniards had escaped execution because Menéndez's marriage to his Calusa wife confirmed a political alliance with south Florida Indians.[10] The Tequestas' decision to save the mutineers as well as their general hospitality convinced Márquez that the Indians should be incorporated into the Spanish Empire. Márquez, who was lavished with gifts and feasts, proclaimed that the Indians wanted instruction in the ways of Christianity, a cross raised in their village, and a mission built in their midst.

When Márquez departed, Tequesta's brother and three or four others departed for Havana in order to observe the Spanish ways firsthand. The Spanish would "treat them very well and keep them entertained and they give them trinkets that they are very pleased with." The Tequestas also seemed to "wish to become Christians . . . and come every day to the church." We do not know whether the Tequestas asked for a political or economic alliance with the Spanish or whether the Tequesta visitors went to Havana for religious instruction or as diplomatic emissaries looking for powerful partners. Nonetheless, the Tequesta chief made his desire for a mutually beneficial relationship clear enough to convince Spanish authorities to risk establishing a permanent foothold at the North Bank.[11]

The Tequesta mission began in March 1567 under the guidance of Father Francisco Villareal. Like other Jesuit missions in Florida, the North Bank enterprise received only nominal financial support from the Crown. Menéndez pardoned seven mutineers in return for their service to the enterprise and paid a few dozen Spaniards to help construct and administer the site. They established a palisaded fort out of "brushwood faggots" at the mouth of the river. Inside the stockade, the Spanish erected a "settlement with twenty eight houses enclosed by their stockade fort," raised a cross, and likely built a chapel. As they did elsewhere in the empire, the Jesuits relied on local Native labor to construct the mission. As a result, at least from the outside, the circular buildings looked like the homes that the Indians had built for centuries in the region. In addition to the Tequesta residents and laborers, the small settlement would ultimately employ two priests, thirty soldiers, a captain, and some carpenters.[12]

The mission briefly confirmed the optimism that led to its construction. Despite its numbers—the missionaries claimed that about 30 Tequesta families or about 180 people lived under their guidance—Villareal had "great . . . satisfaction at seeing that every morning and evening all the Indian men and women, big and little, hastened to the cross to worship it and kiss it with great devotion." Villareal even arranged a stage production of a religious play on the feast day of John the Baptist in order to help indoctrinate the Indians. The production is now widely considered to be the first play to be performed in what is now the United States. This sense of success, however, was short-lived, as the mission seemed more an intrusion than a welcomed addition. The Tequesta children showed up for instruction and declared that they "wish[ed] to become a Christian," but they did not impress the priest. Father Villareal explained that "they have great difficulty in learning the doctrina and accordingly, they do not come to it." After several months of instruction, Villareal could only take credit for baptizing one Tequesta Indian.[13]

The mission suffered from many problems—an endemic shortage of supplies, "a plague of mosquitos," and soldiers who needed more guidance than the Indians, as Villareal often proclaimed. Villareal, however, could not operate the mission without the soldiers. Armed Spanish soldiers commanded obedience, extracted labor, and helped prevent overt rebellion and early martyrdom for the priests. Soldiers also increased demands on the Tequestas to provide food, shelter, and other supplies and initiated many cross-cultural misunderstandings. The Tequestas themselves, however, may have been Villareal's biggest problem. They may have been "very devoted to the cross" and willing to incorporate it into the pantheon of preexisting spiritual beliefs, but they rejected the expected obedience to the Spanish Crown, the prohibition of ancient practices, and many of the obligations that came with their conversions.[14]

The Tequestas' experience with Catholicism mirrored that of Native peoples elsewhere in the New World. Only a small minority of converted Indians abandoned the traditional customs and beliefs of their people. Instead, they turned to the church to augment their existing religious understanding of the world or to obtain cures for sickness. Villareal himself worried about the sincerity of his successes. When the Tequestas were sick, he explained, "they open up readily," which was the case for Chief Tequesta. When his son became ill, he "came to me and said to me through the interpreter that he did not wish to resort to witchcraft but wanted me to pray for him and put a cross on him, and the next day he was better and is healthy." In early January 1568 another "very ill" woman consented to conversion and died shortly after the hastily performed baptism. Seeking baptismal cures for illness, though, hardly required Indians to abandon traditional treatment or beliefs. Native peoples throughout the region used ritual cleanses and baths to cure ailments of both a physical and spiritual nature. However, the missionaries chose to conclude that their cures offered a radically new approach to spiritual and physical ailments and that the Native peoples had accepted Christianity. Family members of one sick infant, for example, consented to baptism with promises that they did so "so that she would go to heaven, if she should die." At the same time, Villareal knew that family members arranged for the assistance of "shamans" after their conversions to Catholicism. Through the short history of the Spanish missions at the North Bank, the Indians blamed the missionaries for interference. After one "little girl . . . showed no improvement" from a baptism, "shamans . . . worked many spells over her, pressing down on her body so that it seemed like they were kneading it." This also failed, and "the shamans said that if I had not touched her, they would have healed her."[15]

Although the Spanish considered their settlement to be a religious outpost, it also served as a trading post for Native Americans in the region. The Spanish brought a host of trade goods (usually metal goods and various foods) that provided the Tequestas with both material comfort and access to the powerful and unknown spiritual world. On several occasions, Spanish officials complained that the Tequestas only feigned interest in Catholicism if they were given food and trade goods. This convinced Villareal that Tequesta conversions lacked sincerity. "I am in doubt whether they do it out of fear, or with a lack of comprehension, or out of some love or desire for some food of corn, which they desire greatly."[16]

In early 1568, as Villareal gathered supplies in Havana, violence erupted at the mission. Although the rebellion's cause remains a matter of speculation, the timing and firsthand accounts reveal the tensions that underlay the mission itself. According to one account, the problems began when soldiers treated the Indians as "if they had conquered them by war." The soldiers' abusive behavior toward the Indians—the extraction of labor and supplies and perhaps acts of sexual and physical violence—proved too much to bear. Villareal's absence, which prevented him from smoothing over the tensions, made things worse. "When the Indians could endure it no longer, they first warned them that they should leave, (saying) that this was not a good land for settling; and when they were not able to settle it by warnings, they decided to kill those whom they could, among the Spaniards and set fire to their own houses and village." Details of the attack differ, but the Tequestas killed at least four soldiers and may have hoped to "kill the rest of the Spaniards." It seems unlikely that they hoped to exterminate the Spaniards. Although the Spanish soldiers emphasized the unbridled destruction, the Tequestas seem to have restrained their violence. Eighteen soldiers were left unharmed even though they were cut off from water and confined in a wooden structure that could easily have been set aflame. Perhaps Villareal's explanation makes the most sense: the entire episode occurred because a soldier killed "an old Indian . . . who had been a chief" for insulting him. The Tequestas may have sought to punish the perpetrating soldiers rather than slaughter all Spaniards indiscriminately.[17]

The Tequestas' desire to punish Spaniards rather than exterminate them became clear after Márquez returned with supplies. The Tequestas allowed the surviving soldiers to evacuate and welcomed the Jesuits back only a few months later. History, though, quickly repeated itself. Shortly after the violent affair, the Spaniards acted on what they called the Tequestas' "good character" and rejoiced when the "chief told me that he and all his vassals wished to become Christians." They rebuilt the mission, as local Indians gathered the wood needed to rebuild the "fort, houses, and a church." Just as they had a few years earlier, the Spanish conflated the Tequestas' desire to be diplomatically "faithful" with their desire to embrace their subservient position within the empire and Catholic faith. When soldiers committed additional transgressions, the Tequestas "broke" the recently established "peace" and the mission ceased to operate. By 1570 Spain and the Jesuits had abandoned the mission "because the Indians had put the Christians under great pressure."[18]

With the mission gone, the Tequestas quickly began to rebuild the North Bank and their relationship with the Spanish Crown. Although mutual mistrust separated them, the Spanish and Tequestas realized that they had much to gain from an alliance. The Tequestas still needed Spanish trade goods, especially with the increased and threatening English and French presence in the Caribbean. The Spanish hoped that the Tequestas would provide safe harbor for their distressed boats and otherwise prevent their European rivals from establishing colonies of their own. The fear of pirates and privateers who plundered trade and altered the balance of power in the region may have been the most important issue for the Spanish. "It would be advantageous to build a fort there for the security of the ships that might have to leave the channel."[19]

For several years, the only communication between the Tequestas and Spanish remained informal and took place off shore. The Tequestas took canoes to meet ships that anchored in the bay and sometimes traveled north to visit Spanish officials in St. Augustine or south to Havana to trade or meet with government officials. On the shore, the Tequestas dealt with various clandestine traders and sea captains who came to the North Bank as they traveled to and from Havana. Although captains tried carefully to navigate the Bahama Channel and take advantage of the Gulf Stream on their journeys, even the most seasoned captains could not always make it through the Florida straits safely. The bay earned a deserved reputation as a magnet for shipwrecks. Some ships capsized on the reefs, and various crews threw goods overboard to lighten their loads and raise their hulls before they crashed into the sandbars.[20]

Spain's concern with the English and English piracy increased its interest in Biscayne Bay and the North Bank. In 1586, shortly after Sir Francis Drake attacked St. Augustine, Spanish sailors revisited Tequesta in search of the British privateer and slaver. There is no evidence that Drake visited the site, but it was one of many places where Spanish officials believed that he could find safe harbor. When the English established the colony of Jamestown, Spain renewed its formal diplomacy with the Tequestas in order to prevent the English from making inroads in the region. In 1607 Tequesta and Spanish officials rekindled their diplomatic relationship during a meeting in St. Augustine. The Tequestas agreed not to "serve [the English] and allow them to come and go as they will." Fears of the English presence near the Miami River would continue for many years, with some historians declaring that Walter Raleigh visited the Tequestas in 1646.[21]

Menéndez and later Spanish leaders repeatedly recognized the threats that shipwrecks and piracy posed to the Spanish Empire. As a result, Spain could not afford simply to abandon its concern for the North Bank. The governor had a watchtower built on Biscayne Bay to help Spanish treasure ships navigate the region and to hinder the efforts of English and other pirating vessels. The Spanish also commissioned and disseminated maps of the region. In 1575, for example, geographer Juan López de Velasco gathered as much information as he could and created an official description of the Miami River. "At the very point of Tequesta," he explained, "there enters into the sea a freshwater river, which comes from the interior, and to all appearances runs from west to east. There are many fish and eels in it. Alongside it on the north side is the Indian settlement that is called Tequesta." The site, he said, retained geographic importance. "A settlement of Spaniards was established here in the year of 15[67], which was abandoned later, in the year of [15]70. They say it would be advantageous to build a fort there for the security of the ships that might have to come out of the [Bahama] Channel and because the land is good for settlement."[22]

Despite the efforts of the Spanish Crown and sea captains, shipwrecks regularly occurred near the North Bank. The Tequestas benefited from the lost cargo, but so did opportunistic sailors from across the Atlantic world. During the late sixteenth century, a clandestine community of sailors effectively hid along the Miami River and in various Keys and nearby waterways. These sailors came from various backgrounds, but most of them were Spaniards who had escaped from the labor arrangements that brought them to the Caribbean. Working outside of the law and on the edges of the empire, they bought, built, or stole small boats and lived offshore along the Florida coast. Some became known as pirates, but these small bands rarely attacked boats at sea. Instead, these opportunistic salvagers camouflaged their illegal activities behind a façade of benign economic

Figure 2. Throughout the sixteenth and seventeenth centuries, the Tequestas obtained captives and trade goods when Spanish and other ships wrecked in Biscayne Bay. This sketch reveals the widespread fear among Spaniards and other Europeans who traveled through the Florida straits. *Florida Indians Capturing Shipwreck Victims* (1707). Black & white photoprint, 8 × 10 in. Printed with permission of the State Archives of Florida, *Florida Memory*, https://www.floridamemory.com/items/show/26221.

pursuits like fishing and turtling and frequently traded goods with the Tequestas in return for access to the river and its fresh water.[23]

The Tequestas' relationship with pirates and survivors of shipwrecks as well as their rejection of the earlier missions earned them a brutish reputation. As ships and crews went missing, Spaniards and other Europeans drew upon anti-Indian stereotypes to imagine the worst. According to one account, the Tequestas would "kill all the people from the [Spanish cargo] ships which are, the most of them, lost in this district." Another somewhat fanciful account stated that the Tequestas used the premise of "gold and silver . . . which they have from the ships that have been lost thereabouts" to lure thirty Spaniards into a house and then killed four of them before the rest escaped. Although there is little evidence that Tequesta Indians actively enticed Spaniards to their shores, they captured many shipwrecked sailors in Biscayne Bay. Indeed, in many instances, the Spanish government had to ransom Spanish captives and their cargoes from the Tequestas. Ransom was not always an option. In 1574 the Tequestas killed five Spaniards, including Captain Alonso de Lobera, when they approached the shore on a frigate. In another instance the Tequestas killed a group of castaways with darts or arrows and clubs, leaving one survivor to tell the tale and otherwise let the Spanish know that their presence was unwanted.[24]

The Tequesta "savages" terrified many of the sailors who passed through the region. Part of the fear came from unsubstantiated reports of cannibalism and human sacrifice, details that they added to distinguish Indian customs from their own "civilized" forms of barbarity. Rather than seeing Tequesta warfare as acts of self-defense, Spanish officials concluded that the Tequestas deserved conquest because they had "blood lust for killing Christians." The link between barbarity and conquest extended throughout the new world, as the Spanish and others used it to wage "just wars" against Native peoples. Indians who practiced cannibalism, human mutilation, and other "savage" acts relinquished their rights to humane treatment. The rejection of the mission may have served as enough proof to justify the conquest of the Tequestas—as did their perceived "worship of the devil"—but the policy toward Spanish castaways sealed the deal. As Menéndez concluded, the Tequestas earned the harsh treatment they received. The Indians were "taught and very well treated," he explained, but they repaid the Spaniards by breaking "the peace many times" and "killing at different times many Christians who were going and coming along the coast in all safety." Therefore, he declared, "it was fitting that they be declared slaves, whereby he could continue the conquest and settlement of that province." Despite Menéndez's argument, the king refused his request for "War [to] be made upon them with all rigor, a war of fire and blood, and that those taken alive shall be sold as slaves, removing them from the country and taking them to the neighboring islands." As a result, the Spanish governor abandoned his plans to conquer or control the Tequestas.[25]

The arrival of the English in the Southeast in the late 1600s ultimately had a dramatic impact on the Tequestas at the North Bank. In south Florida, their impact was first felt through the Indian slave trade. Although Spanish slave raids into south Florida predated León's arrival in 1513, the increased scale of the English slave trade brought a new level of anxiety and upheaval to Native Floridians. In the seventeenth and early eighteenth centuries, thousands of Indians were captured from their Florida homes and shipped to work in the fields of the Caribbean. Raiding Indians—supplied and encouraged by English merchants—captured around 4,000 Native Floridians between the years 1704 and 1706 alone. Countless others lost their lives defending themselves and their families from the raiders. At first, the upheaval remained far from the Everglades and coastal communities like the North Bank. Some survivors from north Florida took refuge among the Tequestas. As the raids slowly made their way deeper into Florida, the Tequestas became refugees as well. Some fled to the Keys and to Havana in order to avoid enslavement, but safety was difficult to find. By 1711 slave raiders were repeatedly threatening the Indians in the Florida Keys. The recurring raids led Tequesta leaders to plead for asylum in 1704, 1732, and 1743 as well as at several other undocumented moments.[26]

The most notable slave raid into south Florida occurred in 1708 when Englishman Thomas Nairne and thirty-three Yamasee Indians marched south from Carolina on a bloody slave raid into south Florida. One eighteenth-century mapmaker described the region as being "Wholly laid waste being destroyed by the Carolinians." The Tequesta community at the North Bank had absorbed many of the refugees from the north and therefore remained a large enough target to justify the assault. If Nairne wanted Indian slaves, he felt "obliged to goe down as farr on the point of Florida as the firm land will permit." His journey into south Florida proved fruitful. "They have drove the Floridians to the Islands of the Cape, have brought in and sold many hundreds of them, and dayly now continue that trade so that in some few years thay'le reduce these barbarians to a farr less number."[27]

The slave raids transformed the North Bank. Even as its original inhabitants suffered at the hands of the raiders, the population swelled with the arrival of the newcomers from Tequesta and other Indian communities in the region. One observer remarked in 1743 that the Indians at the North Bank "are all the remnant of three nations, Keys, Carlos, and Boca Raton. We learned that from another three tribes in addition to these, the Maymies, the Santaluzos, and the Mayacas, which have united [and are] four days' journey away on the mainland, it will be possible to add another hundred souls or a few more." These Indians built a village "at the mouth of the [Miami] river . . . that is, five huts (*chozas*) in which up to one hundred and eighty people were living crowded together between men, women, and children, the [last two of] which made up about half of this number." Many of these refugees had alliances through either trade or participation in other missions, leading one observer to state that most of "the adult men understand and speak Castilian moderately well because of the frequent commerce with the boatmen from Havana." Within decades, the North Bank had become a community of refugees who were allied with the Spanish.[28]

In 1743 the Spanish Crown made a final and short-lived attempt to salvage its south Florida presence at the North Bank and in south Florida more generally. Franciscan missionaries, with the support of Havana, offered salvation and a military presence to defend this amalgam of survivors. According to some reports, the Indians at the North Bank were receptive to the new Spanish mission. With the urging of soldiers, the Indians built a rather large triangular wooden fort and were offered salvation by the missionaries. Once again it is unclear whether the Indians wanted protection from slave raiders, access to trade, or spiritual guidance. Almost immediately, the missionaries complained that the Indians seemed less interested in Catholicism than in getting "supplies and whiskey." The priests complained about the relative paucity of souls to save, the counterproductive influence of Spaniards who came in the area to fish or trade, the Indians' worship of idols, and their insistence on keeping various superstitions. The mission did not last long. In 1743 a raid by Yuchi Indians convinced the Indians and the Spaniards of the futility of the enterprise and the entire mission; the Spaniards and most of the Indians evacuated to Havana.[29]

Two decades after the abandonment of the mission, a small community of Tequesta and other Indians still occupied the North Bank. "The Indians of Ratones and the south part of Florida," William Roberts explained, "cure great quantities of this fish" and have "hats and mats they make of grass and barks of trees." They trade these items "with the Spanish who come from the Havana with European goods for the use of the natives." Threatened by these connections and the widely shared belief that the Indians remained "faithful to Spain," leaders in Georgia and other British colonies encouraged raiders into the region. They had little interest in the area but would still "much rather see the Spaniard wholly excluded from the Florida shore." If the Spanish controlled Florida, the English "trade from Jamaica and the Bahamas" would suffer from "distress."[30]

By the time Spain transferred Florida to Great Britain in 1763, the Tequesta people had lost their coherence as a culture and polity. Once numbered in the thousands, the North Bank's population had dwindled to a few dozen. The remaining inhabitants became known for their dependence on the Spanish and their proximity to the coast. Cartographer Fernán de Martínez and others simply referred to them as generic "Costas Indians"; James Adair referred to them as the "Indians of Cape Florida"; and Bernard Romans similarly concluded that the Miami River people were simply part of the Calusas. Most of the survivors at the North Bank had quietly relocated to Havana and disappeared into the amalgam of the Spanish Empire. Others remained in Florida, likely joining with other Indians in the newly formed Seminole and Miccosukee villages in the interior. The Tequestas ceased to exist as a polity, and for the first time in over a millennium the North Bank briefly was up for grabs.[31]

# GATEWAY TO THE CARIBBEAN

I N 1783 a few dozen British loyalists, fugitive African American slaves, and despondent Native Americans took refuge at the North Bank. This group of "banditti"—as both the Americans and Spaniards called them—anchored their boats slightly upstream and camped at the abandoned Tequesta village. They were not the first ones to take advantage of the buildings, natural resources, and remote location, and the site showed significant signs of use since the Tequestas had left. Mariners, mostly Bahamians, had spent the past two decades extracting natural resources from the area and otherwise treating south Florida as the eastern edge of the Caribbean. They mended and took shelter in the Tequesta homes, gathered timber, produced tar to make their ships watertight, fished, planted and then picked limes from trees growing wild near the water, and otherwise gathered whatever food could be found.[1]

Led by William Augustus Bowles, the group used the North Bank as a staging area for a paramilitary campaign designed to undermine both the Spanish Empire and the United States. While at the North Bank the men fixed their boats and stocked up on water, meat, fruits, and other provisions. They built a small wooden structure on the site, a physical statement of ownership that would ultimately succumb to the elements. Years later, remains of the roughly twelve-foot wooden structure were still there. It may have been part of a stockade or small

Figure 3. William Augustus Bowles and several dozen other refugees established temporary homes at the North Bank during their campaign to reassert British control of Florida. This portrait of Bowles reveals the blending of material cultures that characterized his supporters as well as his own persona. *Painting of William Augustus Bowles* (17—). Black & white photoprint, 10 × 8 in. Printed with permission of the State Archives of Florida, *Florida Memory*, https://www.floridamemory.com/items/show/29727.

building that could keep a small quantity of supplies safe from the elements. Whatever its use, seafarers could see the structure from offshore for many years and used it to guide their boats into the mouth of the Miami River.[2]

Before coming to the North Bank, Bowles had fought as an ensign in the British army during the American Revolution, worked as an Indian trader in north Florida, married both a Cherokee woman and a Creek woman, and spent significant time in the British Bahamas. He would not make the North Bank his permanent home, but he frequently used it to avoid detection by the Spanish and others who were intent on tracking him down. From this temporary hideout, Bowles attracted supporters who traveled with him on his campaigns throughout Florida, unsuccessfully sought trade goods and diplomatic backing for his campaign to retake Florida, and otherwise exploited the riches of Biscayne Bay. In 1788 Bowles proclaimed himself to be "Director General of the State of Muscogee," a position that he created for an independent government of Indians and other dispossessed residents of Florida. Most of his energy focused less on issues of Muscogee governance than on his desire to help Great Britain retake Florida. In particular, Bowles hoped to undermine Creek chief Alexander McGillivray and the trading monopoly of his allied Panton, Leslie and Forbes Company. This company had resident traders throughout Creek Indian society and quickly became an important part of the Spanish regime when Florida returned to its control in 1783.[3]

Bowles ultimately failed to overthrow Spanish rule or end the monopoly of the Panton Company, but it was not for lack of effort. He traveled between the North Bank and the Bahamian ports of Nassau and New Providence on several occasions, but he could never muster the support from the British Crown that he believed he deserved. Bowles did not let this lack of support deter his efforts. In 1788 he left the North Bank and destroyed one of the Panton Company's trading posts in central Florida. In 1791, when Bowles returned to the North Bank from Nassau, he used it as a staging area as he tried to capture St. Marks in north Florida and cripple Spain's control of the ports between Biscayne Bay's Cape Florida and Apalachicola far to the north in the Gulf of Mexico. Bowles's grandiose plan failed. Although he captured Panton's central trading post in Apalachee in north Florida, Bahamian merchants could not fill the commercial void and the Spanish control of the trade remained.[4]

Bowles's actions outraged the Spanish, who put a lucrative price on his head. When Spanish governor Juan Nepomuceno de Quesada learned that Bowles was hiding at the North Bank in 1792, he tried to take direct action. Quesada and other Spanish officials in St. Augustine did not want to expend significant resources in order to settle south Florida, but they could not let the British obtain a foothold in Spanish territory. The issue was tricky for the cash-strapped and somewhat isolated colony. Even though Bowles was technically on Spanish terrain, Quesada did not think that he could send in a military force to capture him. The region was widely known as an extension of the Bahamas and was routinely patrolled by British sailors. Sending a small armada would be expensive and would be deemed an act of war—something that the limited diplomatic importance of south Florida hardly justified. Quesada resolved the issue by sending an unarmed ship to the region under the ruse of carrying official communication with Havana. This type of trip occurred with some frequency, with most boats staying clear of the coastline. Quesada's vessel anchored offshore on March 2, 1793, and the captain "went on shore while the people were filling water." Although Bowles and his known associates were nowhere to be found, the Spaniards were in the right place. They "saw Bowles's old camp where stands two large lightwood posts at about 12 feet distance and about 14 feet high—Seems to have had a piece mortized in on the top and appears to have been the entrance of some old fortification." The captain also found "In the pine barren . . . 2 old tarr kilns" that he believed were used by British soldiers "during the last war." Intent on preventing Bowles from making use of the site again, the Spanish soldiers "set the woods on fire and came on board." The destruction of the site may have convinced Bowles not to return to the Miami River—his whereabouts at this time remain largely unknown—but his paramilitary campaign continued until he was captured in 1804.[5]

Bowles's presence at the North Bank illuminates the major themes that shaped the site's history between 1763 and the early nineteenth century. This period spanned the British occupation (1763–1783) and the Spanish reoccupation (1783–1821) of Florida and witnessed the tumults created by the American Revolution. As these rather well-known stories took place, a different but connected history unfolded at the North Bank. During this era, south Florida was more an informal colony of local Bahamians than it was a formal colony of the British or Spanish Empires. Ad hoc rather than officially sanctioned leaders and settlers controlled the site. As the story of Bowles reveals, life there was largely hidden from outsiders and was more connected to runaway slaves, fugitive whites, and Seminole and Creek Indians than to traditional colonists. With a few exceptions, most of the North Bank's inhabitants were squatters or visitors who stayed too briefly to be described as residents. During the period, the North Bank retained the natural advantages that had earlier lured the Tequestas to the area, but this generation of occupants made a virtue of its isolation from the Americans to the north. They came to the edge of the empire in order to be left alone, which for the most part historians have continued to do.[6]

This lost Bahamian history in Florida began just as the Tequestas evacuated the region in 1763, if not before. As south Florida's Spanish and Tequesta population left, other individuals moved into the structures that they left behind. These newcomers included privateers, pirates, fishers, turtlers, wreckers, loyalists, debtors, and various other fugitives from the Atlantic world. Many of the newcomers fit in more than one of these categories, which were more descriptions of activities than formal occupations. For example, pirates fished, salvaged wrecks, hunted turtles, and lost political fortunes during the revolutionary era. Like Bowles and his supporters, the visitors to the North Bank included Europeans, Indians, and Africans. Most of them were more connected to the Bahamas than they were to mainland North America or northern Florida.[7]

Bahamians and other visitors primarily came to the North Bank for a short time, and sometimes repeatedly, in order to extract resources for use in their journeys or in their home markets. For starters, the seafarers would make their way through the bay in order to get access to lumber, a resource that was in short supply in the Bahamas. They also gathered fresh water from the river and perhaps from a local spring; harvested limes, other fruits, and coontie; hunted turtles, deer, and other small mammals for meat; fished and gathered various shellfish; and took advantage of the generally secure location to repair their ships. Such was the case for one early nineteenth-century visitor, Andrew Ellicott. On his journey through the bay, Ellicott stopped for a couple of days on the Miami River—which he called "Fresh Water River." His crew gathered fresh water and limes from the shore area and hunted for deer and turkey. Ellicott's experiences paralleled those of other seafarers who used the mouth of the river to hide their privateering from colonial officials and to salvage shipwrecks. Some stayed for a few hours, while others stayed for weeks on end. As a group, they formed a continuous presence that colonial officials repeatedly decried as a threat to their respective empires.[8]

The constant presence of the Bahamians turned the North Bank and south Florida into what one observer described "as another island of the Bahamas." This influence has been widely acknowledged in the Keys, but the North Bank's location on the mainland may have camouflaged its connections to the islands. Bahamians did more than just visit and extract goods from the site. They introduced and cultivated various plants, including Barbados cherries, soursops, sapodillas, Spanish limes, and sugar apples. These plants made the North Bank seem more "Bahamian" and further attracted later generations of islanders to come take advantage of the bay's wild resources. These influences convinced historian Helen Muir that "south Florida might as well have been an island joined to the Bahamas by sailboat and custom."[9]

The shipwrecks that the coral reefs attracted proved to be the most lucrative attraction for the part-time Bahamian residents of the North Bank. Throughout the sixteenth through nineteenth centuries, captains traveled the perilous shorelines only to lose their boats and cargo to storms, coral reefs, and sandbars. As one surveyor later explained: "many vessels . . . were lost in fair weather: unacquainted with the stream's eddy, and of foundings being under blue water, they were swept insensibly by the eddy to the westward; and . . . run strait upon a reef." Small and sometimes large fortunes awaited those who were willing to dive into the waters or troll the shores. Greater fortunes could be had by those willing to extort rewards from captains who ran aground and needed a tow to safety or assistance unloading their cargo. Although popular imagery and modern news focus on the lost gold and silver from the Mexican mines, the wreckers and salvagers frequently obtained more mundane booty and fees for rescuing those in need. Salvagers capitalized on everything from the various parts of the ship (anchors, wood, rope, sails, and so forth) to the trade goods (cotton, corn, rice, tobacco, guns, ammunition) and other supplies that often got thrown overboard to lighten loads. This experience continued into the nineteenth century, as the changing of European dominion had little effect. At the turn of the nineteenth century, Ellicott observed that Key Biscayne and the surrounding areas were "much frequented by the privateers, wreckers, and turtlers from the Bahama Islands." A few years later, in 1807, John Aikin explained that Bahamian wreckers took full advantage of "the channels between the Bahamas and the coast of Florida." In some instances, wreckers would burn the ships after the cargo that "they may not serve as a beacon to guide other ships clear of those dangerous shoals."[10]

Although wrecking was not legal in the eighteenth century and captains retained the rights to their flotsam, Bahamians and others skirted the law to make it a part-time profession at the North Bank. When they were in control, British and Spanish naval officers frequently tried to curtail the practice, but they had little luck regulating the coastline. Wreckers typically hid themselves and their booty up the Miami River, waiting out any patrolling naval ships that might visit. Other wreckers proclaimed that they were in the region "turtle hunting," a convenient cover for their illegal operations. Although the actions were deemed illegal, the small but constant community of wreckers did little to chase away visitors. When Ellicott "found several of those privateers, wreckers and turtlers," for example, he was "politely treated." Their interaction proved to be rather commonplace; they talked and traded for salt pork and other goods. Shortly after, Pedro Fornells had a similar meeting with the wreckers and others who squatted at the North Bank and made a living on the bay.[11]

The Bahamians also came to the North Bank to trade with

Seminole Indians who occupied the inland wetlands of south Florida. Native Americans had been migrating into the southern interior for several decades before the Tequestas and other Indians abandoned their ancestral homes on the coast. Some of these newcomers may have learned about the area as slave raiders, and others likely arrived during extended hunting trips. Most of the migrating Indians came from the ethnically diverse and decentralized Creek Confederacy in north Florida, Georgia, and Alabama and created new Seminole communities in and near Lake Okeechobee. After they arrived, the Indians incorporated and allied themselves with remnants and survivors of various communities of diverse ethnic backgrounds. Their villages contained some Calusas from the west coast who chose not to evacuate to Havana as well as hundreds of African Americans who had escaped from slavery. Some Tequestas may also have joined the Seminole villages in the seemingly remote interior.[12]

During these often ignored decades of eighteenth-century south Florida history, Seminoles routinely came to the mouth of the Miami River to obtain the same resources that drew the Bahamians to the shores. They traveled on dugout cypress canoes that could often fit a few dozen adults and transport various supplies up the river. They typically poled their way down the Miami River or hugged the coastline. At the mouth of the Miami River, they fished for manatee and shark, harvested the rare materials that shipwrecks left behind, and traded for Bahamian goods. Although the Panton, Leslie and Forbes Company officially monopolized the trade, Seminoles pursued clandestine options at the North Bank and elsewhere. They traded deerskins, honey, beeswax, dried fish, and various fruits to fishers who offered guns, metal goods, rum, cloth, coffee, and other items that the Seminoles could not produce for themselves. Although the North Bank never became the preferred location for trade, it allowed Seminole hunters and families to play trading firms off of one another and otherwise obtain the best trade goods, prices, and opportunities.[13]

Seminoles also traveled to the North Bank and Biscayne Bay to avail themselves of the wild coontie plants in the region. It is unclear how these Seminoles and other migrants learned to grind

Figure 4. From the eighteenth to the twentieth century, Seminole Indians traveled to the North Bank in dugout canoes in order to trade with its residents, gather supplies, and harvest coontie. *Seminole Indians in a Canoe on the Miami River—Miami, Florida* (1912). Black & white photoprint, 8 × 10 in. Printed with permission of the State Archives of Florida, *Florida Memory,* https://www.floridamemory.com/items/show/28066.

and soak the coontie in order to rinse away its toxins, but they may have learned the skills from the Tequesta or Calusa Indians or from the Bahamian sailors who continued to travel to the Atlantic shore. Coontie in some ways replaced corn as the daily dietary staple. The Seminoles grew corn in their small inland gardens, held the annual Green Corn Ceremony, and told stories about the importance of corn. However, the unpredictability of the rising waters of the Everglades and adjacent Big Cypress Swamp made it nearly impossible to have large-scale cornfields like those that had sustained their ancestors in Georgia and beyond. In addition, the recent and potential mobility of the Seminoles—whose territory would be repeatedly threatened throughout the eighteenth and nineteenth centuries—kept them from investing labor into clearing fields for corn. As a result, coontie played an increasingly large place in their daily diet. Like the Tequestas and other southeastern Indians, the Seminoles harvested the roots from the coastal area and manufactured coontie flour. They used it to make bread, thicken stews, and otherwise augment their diet. They also prepared it as "sofkee"—a warm, thick drink that was historically made of corn and soda ash and consumed throughout day. Their ancestors and later their progeny would use ground or pounded corn, grits, or cornmeal, but coontie served a similar dietary purpose in the absence of cornfields or merchants who could provide dried and ground corn.[14]

Seminoles stopped at the North Bank on their way to the Bahamas, the Keys, Cuba, and other nearby islands. These trips took place in dugout canoes that were sometimes outfitted with sails and connected with other canoes to create catamarans. Seminoles traveled to Havana and New Providence on diplomatic missions and to initiate trade. These travels largely went unrecorded, but there are many tantalizing clues to this largely unexplored history of Seminole travelers. In 1773, for example, a Seminole Indian presented naturalist William Bartram with a piece of tobacco that he received from the governor of Cuba. Bartram also believed that the Seminoles sailed to the Bahamas. One Seminole man traded honey with a merchant in Havana in the following century, and another earned the nickname "Key West Billie" on account of his travels offshore.[15]

African Americans—many of who became known as "Black Seminoles"—also stopped at the North Bank on a voluntary migration to Andros Island and other Bahamian Islands. There they escaped enslavement or reenslavement when they were "carried off by the Bahama wreckers" and "smuggled into the remoter islands." These "Seminole negroes" included a wide range of people of color, such as escaped slaves, members of autonomous free black communities, and the descendants of African and Seminole parents. The migrations swelled in 1807 when the British abolished the slave trade and began to resettle thousands of illegally captured slaves in the Bahamas and continued for many years. By the end of the First Seminole War (1816–1818), a trader noted that the Bay contained "about sixty Indians and as many runaway negroes in search of subsistence, and twenty-seven sail of Bahama wreckers."[16]

Some Africans at the North Bank never made it to freedom. Such was the case for an African American child named Ben, who fled with his family from South Carolina, joined a Seminole community near Tampa Bay, and made his way to Biscayne Bay. To help him escape, his mother hired him out to a sea captain who visited the North Bank, looking for laborers. Ben ultimately arrived in Havana, where he was stolen, imprisoned, and "placed in chains" as a slave. After several decades as a slave, he became a public curiosity when his story and his family's escape to Andros Island became widely known. Tragically, Ben died before he could be reunified with his family. But most "Black Seminoles" who sought refuge in the Bahamas made it safely. Bahamian newspapers and officials recorded the influx of hundreds of Black Seminoles, and a Black Seminole community still exists at Andros Island today.[17]

Despite the bustling community of Bahamians, Indians, and African Americans at the North Bank, European officials frequently overlooked the site. Ignoring the Bahamians and other visitors to the North Bank was an important part of European empire building. European governments took jurisdiction over Indian lands with

the doctrine of discovery and then imposed the notion that ownership of lands extended from the act of "improving" them. Clearing
fields, planting crops, and constructing fences demonstrated more
"mastery" over the lands than did gathering foods, hunting animals,
or building "huts" or homes. Owners lived on the land; squatters
hid on the land. The European definitions disqualified the wreckers
and other temporary residents from owning the lands and therefore
made the North Bank technically unoccupied in the decades that followed the Tequesta evacuation. Europeans also required legal claims,
documents that no Native Americans or newcomers could obtain before the seventeenth or eighteenth centuries. In fact, the British government in St. Augustine, which governed the North Bank as part of
the East Florida colony from 1763 to 1783, worked with the knowledge
that all of south Florida remained legally unsettled and therefore in
need of occupation.[18]

In comparison to the early Spanish who occasionally attempted to
colonize south Florida in the sixteenth and seventeenth centuries, the
British hardly tried at all. British traders and planters focused most
of their energy and budget on the areas in north Florida around St.
Augustine and Pensacola, leaving a power vacuum throughout much
of the peninsula. Rather than taking a direct role in overseeing the
development of south Florida, Great Britain delegated the promotion
and settling of the region to a few prominent families who made
these arrangements in exchange for massive land grants. The British,
and then the Spanish after 1783, issued several land grants to the site
and its surrounding areas, but for more than four decades the grants
went undeveloped and therefore reverted back to the Crown. Nothing
that could be described as permanent construction or development
took place at the North Bank again until the early nineteenth century.

As the British government issued grants in the region, surveyors
John William Gerard De Brahm and Bernard Romans traveled to
south Florida to mark the territory for future generations. The presence of the Bahamian wreckers and various other short-term residents earned the attention of both of these men on their separate 1770
journeys to the North Bank. Romans had little respect for De Brahm,

publicly disparaging his rival for having the "brain of Bedlam" and turning the Florida "peninsula into broken islands." Despite their differences, they both proclaimed that the North Bank was uninhabited. In his 1772 *The Atlantic Pilot*, De Brahm explained that none of the islands or coastal sites that he conflated were "inhabited by any of the human species." Romans, likewise, did not record a settlement on the North Bank and instead briefly explained that at the mouth of the Miami River "are the remains of a savage settlement." He described the Miami River or the "river Rattones" as a "fine stream, pretty considerable, with a little good rich soil on its banks, where many tropical plants grow." Romans concentrated on the maritime and ecological rather than the personal history. He focused on the presence of Caribbean plants like coconuts growing on the shores without concern for the people who may have brought them there.[19]

De Brahm and Romans, though, had good reason to ignore the illegal settlements in the region and thereby create a shared lie. Both traveled to south Florida as surveyors and representatives of the British Empire and as part of a larger ambition of opening the region to what they considered legitimate English settlement. Wreckers and refugees could not be seen as occupants—even if the two cartographers frequently mentioned the presence of the wreckers. The Bahamians hid in plain sight. Like the Indians who needed discovering by Ponce de León, however, the Bahamians could not legally occupy the lands. They extracted rather than improved the lands; they visited rather than inhabited them. The perspective of De Brahm and Romans as surveyors further shaped their discussions of the Bahamians. Ownership of lands occurred through the administration of official titles, an expensive process that required the surveying expertise that they could provide.

As much as they were predisposed and trained not to see occupants, De Brahm and Romans both expended significant amounts of ink describing the region's inhabitants. De Brahm, for example, explained that the site was "constantly visited by the English from New Providence, and Spaniards from Cuba, for the sake of wrecks, madeira wood, tortoise, shrimps, fish, and birds." In addition, he explained the Bahamians left evidence of "fresh encroachments" on the coast. Romans revealed a similar scene. Like De Brahm, he wrote that visitors from the Bahamas and elsewhere in the Caribbean took advantage of the site and the rest of the southeastern coast. Indeed, Romans explained that this had long been the case and that the removal of the Tequestas has made the place safer for squatters and shipwrecked mariners. "The people from Providence [Bahamas], who came here for turtle of Mahogony wood, came always armed, and had frequent brushes with them so that the dislodging of these fierce savages has been of service to navigation. The unhappy sufferer by wreck, who escapes with life, may now be sure of safety."[20]

With the "unoccupied" lands surveyed, Britain issued a series of unfulfilled grants that promised to transform south Florida. Many of the grantees hoped to take advantage of the isolation of the area and otherwise turn it into a refuge for those who did not necessarily have a place elsewhere in the region. John Augustus Ernst, the first "owner" of the North Bank of the Miami River, planned on turning the region into a haven for German and Swiss Protestants who had been swept up in a wave of Pietism that corresponded with and influenced the First Great Awakening in America. In May 1767 the British government granted him 20,000 acres on the north side of the Miami River. The land was largely "pine, marsh and savannahs," "situate[d] on Gulph Sandwich, bound by Rock Bridge River [Arch Creek] North by a Fresh Water River South [Miami River] by Biscay Sound East and by Vacant Land West." In other words, it was located directly on top of the Tequestas' abandoned North Bank village. Ernst, an Englishman of German ancestry, never got his settlement off the ground. Several years after he received the grant, he was still "desirous of having [the lands] located" and mapped. When Bernard Romans finally surveyed the territory, he scoffed at Ernst's land and other poorly planned attempts to settle the region. He "often wondered at the stupidity of people let loose in a certain part of the field of commerce," but he was perhaps more critical of the government's rather noncommittal approach. Indeed, he sarcastically recommended that the British government continue its policy of "laying out the land in *large tracts*, the very thing which proved the means of keeping the country uncultivated."[21]

Other large grants set the stage for potential settlements along Biscayne Bay, but, as Romans predicted, they too failed to materialize. Samuel Touchett, for example, obtained a grant of 20,000 acres on the south side of the Miami River in 1766. He had the land surveyed; but before the lands could be reallocated and improved, he committed suicide under a cloud of mounting debts and accusations of economic impropriety. Jean Daniel Roux obtained an equally significant land grant along Biscayne Bay in 1772, but he too died before he even arrived in south Florida. The Spanish similarly struggled to resettle the region and "improve" the lands after they regained Florida from Great Britain in 1783. In 1794, while Bowles took advantage of the region's isolation, Joseph Collins made another short-lived and underdeveloped plan to settle the Miami area. Until the nineteenth century these "uncultivated" lands remained unsettled in the eyes of the law.[22]

During these years of indeterminate claim, the North Bank site technically had no owner and existed outside of the jurisdiction of the Spanish or English. Although surveyors and others would declare that the North Bank was ready for settlement and that land grants could allow the empire to expand, the site was hardly empty. The North Bank and the surrounding areas were Indian country, squatter country, and an informal extension of the Bahamas or Caribbean. Indeed, hundreds of individuals made temporary homes on the North Bank, struggled to hide their identities and presence from European authorities, extracted natural resources from the region in order to augment their more permanent communities elsewhere, and otherwise refrained from claiming legal ownership over the lands. The contrast with the permanent Tequesta settlement, which Spain had attempted to incorporate into its empire, could not be more apparent.[23]

# BECOMING SOUTHERN

A FEW YEARS AFTER Bowles abandoned the North Bank, the region underwent a transformation that betrays most people's images of early Miami and Florida. By the early 1800s it hosted a large and bustling slave community that was connected to the slave societies of the American South and Caribbean. This community has attracted little attention from the public or among scholars, but in many ways it typified how the enslavement of Africans allowed white owners to amass personal fortunes and connect their provincial lives to the modern world. The cotton that southern planters often described as "white gold" would not flourish on the North Bank, but the tropical fruits from its orchards would find their way to both local and distant marketplaces. The North Bank's most famous antebellum owner would become one of the wealthiest and most powerful planter politicians in the region. Richard Fitzpatrick, like many landlords in the tropics of the American South, owned but hardly occupied the site. Instead, he left the burdens of plantation management and occupation to approximately sixty enslaved Africans and an overseer tasked with extracting their labor and obedience. Miami's experience with African slavery was fleeting, however, and was largely over only a few decades before Indians wars would usher in a new form of settlement in the region.[1]

The movement toward plantation life and the imposition of deeded property began in 1806 when John Egan (sometimes Hagan) migrated from St. Augustine to south Florida and made his home on the North Bank. It is unclear whether he was married at the time, but ultimately he would share the property with his wife, Susan, and a son. When Egan left East Florida's capital, a small group of St. Augustine's merchants and planters had already begun to connect Florida's economy to the Atlantic world. These boosters built their dreams on the promise of distant trade markets, the dispossession of Indian lands, and the unpaid labor of enslaved Africans. The North Bank, however, differed remarkably from most of the other settlements in Spanish East Florida, for it was far from the authorities in St. Augustine that directly oversaw its development, which allowed the North Bank to operate autonomously from colonial officials. This isolation would continue after Spain ceded sovereignty over Florida to the United States in 1821, as territorial authorities struggled to regulate affairs in the stretch of lands that connected to the colonial capitals of St. Augustine and Pensacola.[2]

South Florida's Native American population, at least at the start of the nineteenth century, was also smaller and more remote than many of the communities to the north. Although Seminole and Miccosukee Indians occupied the southern part of the peninsula long before Egan did, most of the Indians remained inland and north of Lake Okeechobee, where they contested the territorial claims of Spain and then the United States. Those in the south primarily occupied the interior wetlands and only occasionally went to the coastal region to trade with visiting sailors or, perhaps more important, to harvest coontie. By the time Egan arrived, the southern part of Florida was known for its abundance of coontie.[3]

Miami's proximity to the Bahamas and Havana also connected its inhabitants with material resources that were somewhat rare in the northern part of Florida. As a result, the North Bank associated with the neighboring islands of the Caribbean more than with the Spanish settlements in northern Florida. It received immigrants, trade goods, and news from the east and south more than from the north.

The Bahamian influence in Miami began with the wreckers of the earlier generation, but it continued with the arrival of Egan and other settlers and had much to do with geography. The Bahamas lay only about 185 miles offshore from Miami. In comparison, a bit more than 300 miles separated the North Bank from St. Augustine. Egan, like many of the white migrants who followed him to the region and many of the enslaved Africans who toiled there, migrated indirectly or directly from the not-so-distant Bahamian colony. Indeed, as Egan claimed title of the North Bank in 1808, several other Bahamians obtained Spanish land grants near and along the Miami River, while others remained in the area as squatters.[4]

The Bahamian influence extended to the ecological similarities and limitations of the two regions. Despite the ambitions in both areas, planters never quite mastered the ability to cultivate cotton, indigo, rice, tobacco, or the other staple agriculture products that defined slavery throughout most of the Americas. Instead, planters in south Florida and the Bahamas typically focused their efforts on the extraction of natural resources—often orchards or "wild" plants that were cultivated and augmented by European newcomers but pre-dated their arrival. In these communities, the slave economies were extractive in nature; they depended on the exploitation of existing resources rather than on the intensive agriculture that typified slavery in most of the Caribbean and American South.[5]

Egan's English background hardly limited his ability to obtain land in Spanish East Florida. In 1783, as the British ceded Florida back to Spain, many of its English-speaking residents and refugees fled to the disparate corners of the British Empire. A large number went to the Bahamas, but hundreds remained in Florida, where the Spanish welcomed them into their communities. In the 1790s Spain offered land grants to non-Spaniards willing to occupy and settle sparsely settled parts of Florida. These settlers obtained land in return for loyalty to the Crown and nominal allegiance to the pope. This policy was pragmatic, to say the least. Spain did not want to allocate the resources to fund settlements and, unlike England, did not have a glut of landless people willing to take on the risk of overseas colonization.

In this context, Egan's migration southward makes sense. By following the avenue of advancement that the Spanish Crown opened for English people like him, Egan could dream of material riches and maintain his imperial allegiance.[6]

Egan, like other settlers in south Florida, hoped that the distance from imperial control would allow him to start his life afresh. James had good reason for his optimism. Egan apparently arrived in south Florida as one of a few "respectable pilots at Cape Florida." He lacked the legal right to settle the lands, but the natural resources of the river and Biscayne Bay captivated him. He "squatted near Miami river" and quickly sought to legitimize his stay. Within two years of his arrival, Egan obtained a 100-acre land grant to the North Bank from Spain: the captain-turned-squatter obtained the first private title to the property.[7]

For Egan and his wife and the early nineteenth-century migrants to south Florida, the region seemed to be the next frontier, the next place where opportunities existed through the availability of land. Cheap land did not guarantee success, however, and proximity to the Bahamas hardly guaranteed reliable access to supplies. The Egans and other settlers in the region hoped to find an easily exportable surplus crop, but the mangroves and calcium-rich bayfront terrain hardly offered an easy solution. He experimented with cotton and sugar, but the crops that fed the region's export economies did not flourish. Egan struggled to obtain laborers, enslaved or free, to suit his ambitions. In the end, he purchased and hired enough slave labor to make a living by harvesting and selling limes, coconuts, and bananas from the trees that the Spanish missionaries and the Bahamian mariners had cultivated. Despite his best efforts, Egan primarily expanded and profited from the crops that the earlier generations of settlers on the North Bank had left behind.

During his first few years in Miami, Egan remained physically and economically connected to the planter community in St. Augustine, making several round trips to St. Augustine. On an 1812 trip, he witnessed some of the tumultuous events known as the Patriot War, an attempt by private citizens of the United States with the aid

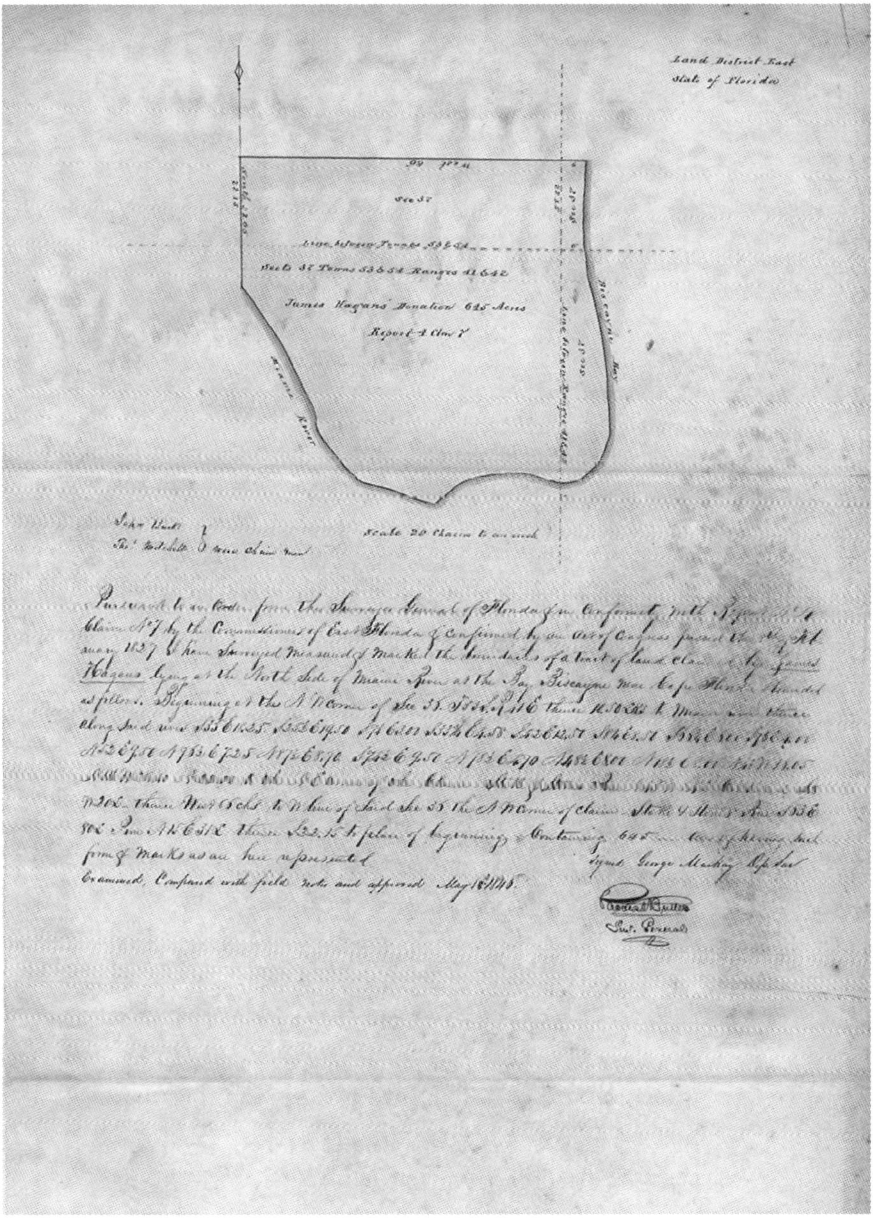

Figure 5. Although he was not its first resident, John Hagan (also Egan) obtained the European land grant to occupy the North Bank of the Miami River. His grant was officially confirmed and transferred years later after the United States took sovereignty of Florida. James Hagen (Hagan) Land Grant (1808), Spanish Land Grants, Box 16, Folder 8. Printed with permission of the State Archives of Florida, *Florida Memory*.

of some Native American allies to annex Spanish Florida as part of the new nation. Egan wanted nothing of it. He likely shared the belief of many English settlers, who felt that the new war threatened the economic and political liberties that accompanied Spanish rule. In December 1812 Egan briefly opposed these insurgents on the St. Johns River as a "master of a small schooner." He expressed shock at the destruction that slaveholding homesteads suffered at the hands of the insurgents and watched as his former neighbors abandoned their homes and "US and Patriot troops were raising the devil on Richard Isabella's plantation." He later explained that the invasion "had broken everybody up," by destroying the stable and profitable society that had emerged there for English speakers and Spanish speakers. The war created tremendous upheaval but not independence, as East Florida remained under Spanish rule. It would take the First Seminole War (1816–1818) to convince the Spanish to relinquish their hold on Florida.[8]

Shortly after the Patriot War, Egan left his career as a ship captain and became more committed to exporting the coconuts and limes that grew on the mature trees at the North Bank. He also planted and then harvested bananas and other fruits. He staked rows of new trees, poking holes into the thin layer of soil and limestone under the property. Egan quickly learned that agriculture was largely out of the question. The greenery of the mangroves fooled many newcomers, who presumed that the cypress trees and underbrush could simply be replaced by desirable agricultural commodities. Rather than hiding rich soil, though, the mangroves obtained their nutrients from the waters that covered a porous but calcium-rich limestone underbelly. One of Egan's neighbors to the south, for example, discovered the lack of topsoil the hard way. "A gentleman at Cape Florida . . . had cut down trees with the intention of clearing a field to plant," one visitor explained. "In order to get rid of the trees which had been felled, in an expeditious manner, he set fire to them, and on the following morning was greatly surprised to find that he had not only destroyed the trees, but had also burnt off the whole of the soil, and left nothing but the bare rocks." In this environment, the limestone and a thin layer of soil could provide stability and nourishment for the root structures of coontie plants and various fruit trees in ways that they could not easily provide for cotton plants and sugarcane.[9]

Despite these limitations, the small community around the North Bank became increasingly stable in the early nineteenth century. This stability continued even as the territory experienced the upheaval of the First Seminole War, which largely confined itself to the north, and Spain's 1821 transfer of Florida to the United States. The changing of the flags had little effect on Egan and his neighboring landowners, at least on a day-to-day basis. Although many residents in the northern part of the colony evacuated, the United States offered the residents of south Florida a reason to believe that the region was on the threshold of booming. Indeed, the United States sold its newly acquired territorial lands on the cheap to those willing to settle there, as part of federal ambition to improve the territory. To support this growth, the United States acknowledged the legality of properly established Spanish land grants and funded the construction of a lighthouse at Cape Florida in Biscayne Bay. The lighthouse would not be completed until 1825, but its construction fed the region's optimism about a commercial future.[10]

The Egans quickly took advantage of his earlier land claims, applied to have their deeds validated by the United States, claimed surrounding acreage, and otherwise watched as English-speaking Americans migrated into the coastal area with dreams similar to their own. Not surprisingly, the Egans used their ecological knowledge of the region and expanded their holdings to the richer soils of the interior. They also consolidated control over the mouth of the Miami River by claiming lands on the south bank. In 1821, almost immediately after the United States claimed sovereignty over Florida, Egan's son James attained a 640-acre homestead that bordered the North Bank's tract and Susan obtained a 640-acre homestead on the south side of the river. The Egans settled and "improved" these lands as well as the land that they held from the Spanish land grants for several years before finalizing the land claims on December 27, 1825. At the same time, several other planters joined the Egans on the river and bay.[11]

As with many Florida dreams, however, Egan's fell flat. He owned lands that could not support agriculture and lived along a river that attracted sailors but not lucrative commerce. The lighthouse helped some sailors traverse the coastline, but one lighthouse hardly protected sailors from the unpredictable winds, plentiful reefs, and sandbars that lay just offshore. Like many others who had harbored Florida dreams, Egan eventually abandoned his and decided to sell his land near the end of the 1820s. An advertisement in the *Key West Register and Commercial Advertiser* in February 1829 described the property's potential while admitting that the only known assets had ancient roots. "The land is very good," Egan boasted in the ad. "There is at present a number of bearing Banana and Lime Trees, and the fruit is inferior to none raised on the Island of Cuba. Any Person desirous of purchasing a Valuable Plantation will do well to visit the Land." In addition, Egan proclaimed that an industrious farmer should be able to "produce Sugar Cane or Sea-Island Cotton, equal if not superior to any other part of the Territory." Like many Miami hucksters, Egan promised potential investors exactly what they hoped to hear—a relatively cheap opportunity to enter the booming slave economy. Yet, even as the ad pushed the promise of coastal agriculture, it revealed Egan's own failure to create a sugar plantation that rivaled those in the Bahamas or elsewhere.[12]

As much as Egan and others promoted the region's future in sugar and cotton, his property did not sell quickly. Egan could not point to past profits. Even the geography of the location was largely unknown to prospective buyers. Surveyors and others, for example, disagreed over the measurable aspects of the locale; they debated the length of the river, the location of its falls, and the navigability of the neighboring Everglades. In addition, they offered contradictory accounts of virtually everything—including the arability of the land, its suitability for agriculture, and the presence of Indian neighbors. Newcomers concluded that they could not trust locals. Local inhabitants, for example, told cartographer John Lee Williams that the "altitude" of the glades was 40 feet. Williams was unconvinced and instead declared it to be unknown. Even after visiting the lower east coast in 1828, he wrote: "The Miame River is a small stream that issues out of the glades and enters Sandwich Gulf behind Cape Florida. . . . The height of the glades above the tide has not been ascertained." While settlements surrounded the North Bank, the interior remained largely unknown. It still belonged to the Seminoles, and fears about their martial prowess and hostility to strangers curtailed many efforts to explore the interior.[13]

The Egans eventually found a buyer in Richard "Fizzy" Fitzpatrick, one of the most powerful men in Key West. Fitzpatrick, like most white people in Florida, was not native to the territory but rather a migrant from elsewhere. In his own words, he was "brought up a planter" from Columbia, South Carolina, and in Miami he pursued the agricultural and commercial ambitions that typified this background. The actual date that Fitzpatrick took possession of the 640 acres on the North Bank is not known, but the property likely changed hands in December 1830. "Fizzy" bought it for four hundred dollars and followed up the transaction by purchasing adjacent lands on the north side of the river and a similarly sized plot on the south. By 1835 he had purchased approximately 3,300 acres for $2,690. In a short time, he would be the largest private landholder in sparsely settled south Florida.[14]

Unlike most white settlers in south Florida, Fitzpatrick came to the region with significant resources. Like many of the other white settlers, however, he probably came to the region to escape the restrictions of his birth. Although surrounded by all of the privileges of slaveholding wealth, he was also surrounded by scandal. When he was a young child, his parents separated. While they fought over their estate in court, his father took on a significantly younger mistress and took no pains to hide it. When they had an out-of-wedlock child together, the entire family became social pariahs in the close-knit community of elite Carolinians. After his father died, a messy legal fight ensued. Fitzpatrick walked away with a sizable estate of land, cash, and slaves. The 1810 census listed the 18-year-old Richard Fitzpatrick as the owner of sixty slaves and a plantation just outside of Columbia. Although he was one of the wealthiest members of the community, he fled Columbia within a few years and briefly traveled the world as a "man of moving habits."[15]

In 1822, shortly after Key West came under the control of the United States, Fitzpatrick moved there. He brought his financial wealth and "reputable" upbringing with him, even as he tried to leave his scandalous family history behind. Like many others, Fitzpatrick used the unsettled nature of the Florida frontier and his considerable wealth to re-create his public identity. He could not change his past, but he could rewrite it. In this regard, Fitzpatrick was like many other settlers of the Florida peninsula who treated early nineteenth-century Florida as a "Paradise for Rogues." Fitzpatrick did not have to rewrite his past completely, but in Key West and elsewhere in Florida he could expect little interrogation about his familial shortcomings.[16]

Fitzpatrick quickly became a valued participant in Key West's wrecking business—the economic engine of the small community. With his inherited wealth, he entered the business at the very top. He purchased and staffed a wrecking boat called the *Eagle* as early as 1825 and later operated a schooner called the *Florida*. Fitzpatrick augmented the profits from his wrecking ventures by becoming the official auctioneer in Key West, creating alliances with local and distant politicians, and otherwise taking on local governmental posts. He became a significant source of capital for struggling neighbors in need of loans, made his share of local economic and social rivals, and otherwise pursued a myriad of economic opportunities. He also purchased lands on the New River in what is now Ft. Lauderdale, which he promptly rented to William Cooley and other aspiring farmers and wreckers. He hired laborers to harvest lumber from unsettled properties that he did not own. Although this action seemed to defy the law, Fizzy escaped conviction for this theft in a local court. Finally, he imported "an intelligent, educated colored man named Hart . . . from the Bahamas" to introduce the salt-making industry to Key West.[17]

Fitzpatrick never lost sight of his planter roots. Even as he enjoyed a healthy profit from his various ventures, he turned his attention to Egan's faltering property at the North Bank. Like many other elite southerners, Fitzpatrick recognized that land was not simply an essential part of any agricultural enterprise. It was also a valued asset itself, and its value could be manipulated through the spread of information on the speculation market. Fitzpatrick connected these two ambitions. He sought to connect the North Bank to the emerging slaveholding empire in the region and otherwise reestablish his place atop the southern hierarchy. Working as a planter would provide him the respectability that he needed for political stature and, he hoped, expand his already formidable economic holdings. The isolation of South Florida made it the perfect place for such ambitions, as Fitzpatrick would join a long list of antebellum Americans who discovered that in recently created Dade County "the administration of the law . . . was worse than a farce."[18]

Fitzpatrick's purchase of the North Bank and other south Florida lands seemed largely about improving the value of his holdings for the speculation market. This financial game was repeated across the U.S. frontier, as entrepreneurs gambled that they could turn profits on the increasing but unrealized values of Indian lands and other territories not yet under official cultivation. As historian Edward Baptist explained: "Southwestern and northeastern entrepreneurs were using the allure of investment in future commodity frontiers developed by enslaved labor, and in the process they created a national financial market for land speculation." As the holder of surplus acreage, any substantial increase in the value of the lands could provide a nice profit if buyers could be found.[19]

With the optimism and disdain for the truth that was typical of land speculators, Fitzpatrick raved about the quality of North Bank's land. In 1831, shortly after he bought the property, he actively pushed the legislature to create an official survey of south Florida and then immediately promoted the region for its "abundance of fine timber suited for naval purposes." Selling south Florida, though, required more than describing the known terrain. To sell its potential, Fitzpatrick relied on his personal reputation. His background from the South Carolina elite, he proclaimed, made him both a knowledgeable and trustworthy predictor of the future. "This Country (South Florida) has heretofore been considered as of no value, but a single look at the map is sufficient to convince any intelligent man . . . there are good lands to be found there. . . . I have seen more of the country than any white man in Florida, one other excepted, and being brought up a planter in South Carolina it is natural to suppose I must know something of the quality of land and its fitness for cultivation." As he boasted of the lands, though, he necessarily highlighted the improvements made by the Tequestas and Spanish settlers before him. "You will no doubt be surprised when I state to you this fact that the Lime and Banana trees grow here in the greatest perfection as well as the sugar cane which is never injured by frost and grows from year to year until cut." This description of sugarcane included claims that would be betrayed in the years that followed, but it helped readers imagine south Florida as part of the emerging plantation South.[20]

Like many privileged planters in undesirable climates and regions, Fitzpatrick eventually used his considerable means to become an absentee landlord. He relied on overseer James Wright to supervise and extract the labor of roughly sixty African slaves on his south Florida holdings. Although he may have purchased some of these slaves from Florida's slave markets or from the Bahamas, Fitzpatrick seems to have transported most of his enslaved workers from South Carolina. Once in Miami, Wright put them to work harvesting the tropical fruits that proliferated on the North Bank and clearing the interior lands in order to grow cotton and sugarcane. Like overseers elsewhere in the region, Wright was responsible for pushing the enslaved Africans to maximize their labor and otherwise keep them "hard at work."[21]

Little is known about the sixty enslaved Africans who lived and died at the North Bank on Fitzpatrick's land. From the scant records left and the analogous communities elsewhere in the region, a few important details emerge. First, in part because Fitzpatrick could not focus on cotton or monoculture, the slaves performed a wide range of tasks. In addition to cooking their own food and tending to the daily needs of their owner, their overseer, and their own community, they tried to grow sugar and other crops; herded cattle; tended to other domesticated animals; picked oranges, limes, and olives; and experimented with various agricultural pursuits. They also helped cultivate and mill coontie, which Fitzpatrick shipped north for upward of eight cents a pound. Their tasks obviously matched Fitzpatrick's restlessness as he struggled to find a treasured commodity. Second, Fitzpatrick rented out some of his slaves to neighbors. By 1840 the recently established Dade County had swelled to 446 mostly free residents, but only a few brought enslaved workers with them. Fitzpatrick capitalized on these newcomers who needed extra hands to clear lands, plant trees, or build homes. In this manner, Dade County began as a slave community without many slaveholders. As Fitzpatrick's workers routinely traveled up and down the Miami River and Biscayne Bay, they created tremendous anxiety. When the Second Seminole War began in 1835, a frustrated Fitzpatrick declared that his slaves seemed eager to fall "into the hands of the Indians." Evacuating them required that he use "great exertions."[22]

Fitzpatrick's ownership of the Miami River property placed him in a good position to make money in real estate. He needed the help of the territorial politicians, however, to make it a reality. Not surprisingly, then, his purchase of the North Bank coincided with the start of his controversial career in Florida's territorial politics. He served several terms in Tallahassee as representative from Monroe County (which included Key West) and then Dade County between 1830 and 1838. When he was briefly out of office, he served as justice of the peace and remained active in territorial affairs. These positions opened opportunities to take a prominent role in various insurance companies as well as in a private attempt to use governmental money to build canals in south Florida. Throughout his time in Tallahassee, Fitzpatrick vigorously pursued his personal economic interests. If his slaves could not increase the value of his Miami River estate, perhaps his political power could. In 1835, as a member of the Legislative Council of Territorial Florida, Fitzpatrick introduced a bill to create the South Florida Land Company, "a corporation with the power to buy and sell land in South Florida . . . with the belief that the corporation would ultimately lead to increased" land purchases. The South Florida Land Company bill passed the Legislative Council, but territorial governor John H. Eaton vetoed the bill, suggesting that land companies threatened citizens because they "engross the most valuable lands, and finally establish a system of tenantry." Fitzpatrick, of course, disagreed, as the system that it would have created would have garnered him a tremendous profit.[23]

Scandals, though, characterized Fitzpatrick's political career. In 1835 he won his seat even though his opponent levied accusations of election fraud against him. Although the veracity of the claims remains cloudy, by all accounts he was outvoted in Key West but decisively won the "non-secret" votes to the north. Cooley, his renter and political ally, counted the votes. The accusations of wrongdoing hardly limited Fitzpatrick's political rise in territorial politics. By the end of his career, he had risen to the very top. He served as president of the Legislative Council and attended the St. Joseph's constitutional convention that wrote the future state of Florida's founding document in 1836. Before resigning his seat at the convention, he cast the only vote against ratification—a vote in "solemn protest" again the constitution's approach to banking.[24]

The real setback to Fitzpatrick's plan to entice planters to the Miami River area was the outbreak of the Second Seminole War. Fitzpatrick had long viewed his position in Tallahassee as the key to his future success, and the wartime turmoil made his career path ever more clear. He left the North Bank at the outset of the war and abandoned his hopes of turning it into a southern plantation. Instead, Fitzpatrick became "a valuable and efficient" aide-de-camp and quartermaster to General Richard K. Call from September 1836 to December 1837 and otherwise tied his future to the wartime politics. Fitzpatrick's hopes for transforming the North Bank had ended.[25]

# THE ARMED OCCUPATION
# OF FORT DALLAS

O N JANUARY 6, 1836, Indian warriors raided William Cooley's homestead on the New River in what is now Ft. Lauderdale. Within minutes they killed Cooley's wife, children, and a tutor before liberating two enslaved African Americans in an event that white Floridians quickly decried as the "Cooley Massacre" or "New River Massacre." Word of the attack quickly spread to Fitzpatrick's homestead on the North Bank. Separated by only a few dozen miles by water, the two communities were tightly connected socially and politically. Cooley and Fitzpatrick's relationship extended beyond that of landlord-tenant. They were also political allies, trading partners, and trusted colleagues. Upon hearing of the raid, overseer James Wright evacuated the North Bank with approximately sixty slaves and fled to safety, ultimately taking refuge in the storm-damaged lighthouse at Cape Florida. Fitzpatrick's neighbors did likewise, as the rapidly evacuated coastline became a militarized zone. For the next few decades, the official owners of the North Bank rarely occupied it.[1]

The evacuation of Fitzgerald's plantation occurred at the outset of the Second Seminole War (1835–1842). The war began as part of the United States policy of "Indian removal" and the larger process of the "western expansion" of the nation. For Florida's Indian communities, what was euphemistically called "removal" and "expansion" felt more like a brutal program of ethnic cleansing, whereby they saw their homelands desecrated, villages burned, and political leaders delegitimized. For white Americans, dispossessing Indians of their lands did more than open up millions of acres to cotton production and African slavery; it also helped alleviate fears that escaped African American slaves would forge alliances with Seminoles and other southeastern Indians. In 1823 and 1832 these forces ultimately led the United States to negotiate removal treaties of dubious authority with Native Floridians. These treaties obligated the Indians to move deeper into the peninsula and ultimately west to Indian Territory.[2]

Most Indians in Florida rejected the legitimacy of the agreements and refused to move west. The raid of Cooley's home occurred as Seminoles killed many of the chiefs and United States agents that they blamed for deceitfully arranging these treaties. In the most widely reported events, they killed agent Wiley Thompson and Seminole chief Charlie Emathla for orchestrating and enforcing the 1832 Treaty of Payne's Landing. At the same time, Seminole warriors also attacked General Francis Dade's command as it marched through Indian lands on the way from Tampa to Fort King. Violence was sporadically popping up across Florida in 1836, and many settlers sought safety elsewhere. When the violence initially threatened his North Bank homestead, Fitzpatrick recalled that he felt "obliged to abandon the plantation, leaving everything behind him except the negroes." He left his overseer and slaves behind to tend to the damage done by a recent hurricane before they too abandoned the site when violence manifested itself at the New River.[3]

The Seminoles' decision to attack Cooley's homestead—like the more renowned sparks of the Second Seminole War—resulted from a deep sense of personal duplicity. For the past decade, Cooley had traded with the local Indians—providing them with locally produced coontie flour and various necessities that he could obtain through the Atlantic trade. Cooley offered metal knives, copper kettles, guns, ammunition, and alcohol in exchange for deerskins, alligator pelts, and various wild fruits and vegetables that the Seminoles harvested in the interior. Cooley, however, was not a typical trader. Unconnected to any of the major trading houses, he primarily obtained his goods from Fitzpatrick or from shipwrecked boats off the Florida coast. Cooley made up for his unreliable access to imported trade goods through hospitality and other acts of reciprocity. In addition, like many Indian traders, Cooley tied himself to his Native American customers through marriage. Cooley's "white" wife, according to several accounts, had lived among the Seminoles for many years. She served as Cooley's interpreter and used her kinship connections to attract Indian customers. At the same time and with the help of Fitzpatrick, Cooley also became a local power broker, serving as justice of the peace of the underpopulated New River community.[4]

In the months prior to the war, Cooley struggled to balance his position as a trusted Indian trader with his obligations as a justice of the peace. When local white settlers murdered Chief Alibama in 1835, Cooley identified the two men responsible and Seminoles hoped that he could obtain justice. When the charges were dropped in county court on account of insufficient evidence, the timing could not have been worse. Cooley's failure fed widespread fears among the Seminoles that their trusted Indian agents and traders were betraying them. In this case they assumed that Cooley must have intentionally withheld evidence to appease his Florida constituents. Shortly after the charges were dropped, the Seminoles from Chief Alibama's camp retreated from the coast and resettled in the interior near Lake Okeechobee. They, like many other Florida Indians, relocated to more defensible areas rather than adhere to the questionable removal treaties.[5]

The onset of war redirected the history of the North Bank. Although Fitzpatrick kept legal title over the property when the fighting began, his and most of the surrounding "settlements were all abandoned to the mercy of the savages." Fitzpatrick ceased being a planter and took his turn at being a soldier. Fitpatrick's participation in the Second Seminole War—like that of many other Floridians—was largely undistinguished. Indeed, United States soldiers frequently complained about the unrealistic expectations, lack of discipline, and unpreparedness of Florida's militiamen. Fitzpatrick hardly broke the stereotype. His lack of formal military training led several military officers to take pains to explain that Colonel Fitzpatrick is "of the legislative council (and not of the army)." Fitzpatrick enjoyed greater influence through his diplomatic efforts. In the winter of 1839–1840, after a string of unsuccessful campaigns to subdue the Seminoles, Fitzpatrick obtained national notoriety for importing Cuban blood-hounds to "discover the lurking places of the Indians." Fitzpatrick did not make the decision to use bloodhounds—Governor Richard K. Call did—but he was an obvious choice to implement that plan. Call trusted Fitzpatrick because they were political allies who were both connected to Andrew Jackson and the Democratic Party. Like many of his less politically connected neighbors, Fitzpatrick also had a se-ries of personal and professional relationships across the Caribbean. Through his connections in Cuba, Fitzpatrick purchased thirty-three bloodhounds (for $151.72 each) to perform reconnaissance and scour "the hiding places of the Seminoles." Fitzpatrick became known for being "most conversant with the mode of keeping and using them," a reputation that earned the scorn of abolitionists, who saw the mili-tary's use of bloodhounds as proof that slavery corrupted the military and nation.[6]

Shortly after Fitzpatrick abandoned his property on the North Bank, the United States military repurposed it and renamed it in honor of Alexander James Dallas, the naval commander who pa-trolled the Florida coast during the war. The officers militarized Fort Dallas for many of the same reasons that Fitzpatrick coveted the property. Officers praised its location on a high bluff that overlooked the mouth of a river and Key Biscayne; some appreciated that it was on an "important canoe route connecting Biscayne Bay and the Ever-glades"; and others understood the value that its trees had for naval ships that needed "to procure wood." Some advantages had to do with the resources that Fitzpatrick had introduced or cultivated on the site. Fitzpatrick's homestead was still standing and offered lum-ber; coconut, lime, and other fruit trees; acres of sugarcane, corn, pumpkins, and sweet potatoes; domesticated hogs and poultry; vast

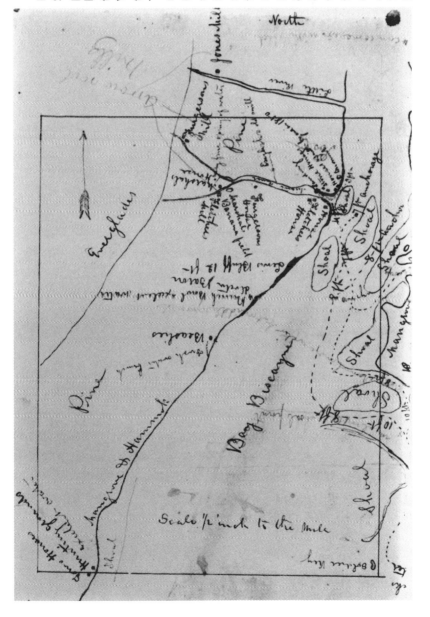

Figure 6. The United States military repurposed Fitzpatrick's homestead during the Second Seminole War and renamed the site Fort Dallas. This detailed map marks several of the notable neighbors and structures, including the landing and stone buildings on the North Bank. Early map of the Fort Dallas area (18—?). Black & white photoprint, 8 × 10 in. Printed with permission of the State Archives of Florida, *Florida Memory*, https://www.floridamemory.com/items/show/36262.

coontie plantings; several abandoned boats; more than a dozen buildings; and a variety of tools and other imported resources that could
be exploited. Not content with these vast resources, the military further developed the North Bank. Joseph Johnston, who later earned
notoriety in the Mexican and Civil Wars, surveyed the area in 1836 in
order to build a blockhouse to serve as the fort's citadel. The military
added other "buildings . . . solidly constructed of stone" to make the
site more suitable for occupation. They dug a well, planted additional
fruit trees, and otherwise created "a pleasant situation . . . where the
married soldiers' quarters, officers homes, storehouses, and gardens
gave a 'village like appearance to the post.'" Despite these additions,
Fitzpatrick's homestead remained more a homestead than a fortification. As Abner Doubleday would later recall from his visits years later,
"There were no fortifications of any kind but it seems to be customary
to call every spot in Florida . . . occupied by a garrison a Fort."[7]

Fort Dallas's role in the Second Seminole War typified the role of
other south Florida forts. Initially, the United States focused most of
its attention on the contested lands in northern and central Florida.
In the south, it sought to isolate the Seminoles by stopping the "illicit
trade being carried on by water between the Main land of Florida, the
Island of Cuba and the Bahamas" and by intercepting "all communication between the Indians and the fishing and other boats from the
Islands of the Bahamas or Cuba." Within a couple of years, as more
Seminoles retreated to the interior of the southern peninsula, the
army took over the fort to stage operations into the Everglades. From
Fort Dallas, the army surveyed the interior, and set out to give "every
annoyance to the hostile Indians" and "harass the enemy as much
as possible." By 1838, the transformation of the North Bank from
a plantation to a military post was complete. The number of men
typically stationed at the fort increased from a few dozen to 126, and
many other soldiers temporarily stopped there on their way toward
the Florida interior.[8]

The soldiers at Fort Dallas—despite its seemingly ideal location on
the "left bank"—did not experience many military successes. Most ex-
cursions returned home without engaging the enemy and with little

to report. In 1841, for example, soldiers left Fort Dallas with hopes of finding Abiaka (Sam Jones), who "left last *Green Corn Dance* for the Hunting Grounds." As the soldiers struggled to track down Abiaka or the enemy more generally, a frustrated guide discovered an Indian camp that was abandoned upon his approach. The soldiers arrived too late to engage the enemy who fled by canoe, but they took solace in their capture of a "hastily abandoned canoe" and the wholesale destruction of a "[swamp] cabbage hammock & pumpkin field." This campaign was more successful than most. Dozens of other expeditions found nothing but long-abandoned camps. Indeed, the inability to find the enemy contributed to a morale problem at Fort Dallas. Local ecological conditions—a prevalence of mosquitoes, horseflies, and hot summers—further frustrated soldiers who found themselves fighting a war that dragged on for much longer than they anticipated. As a result, Fort Dallas struggled with a seemingly continuous stretch of soldiers who were briefly placed "in arrest," put "in confinement," or facing "court martial" for a myriad of offenses that were born of boredom and isolation.[9]

The inability to track down the enemy led the military to wage war on the Indians by preventing them from eating. This adhered to James Gadsden's 1833 belief that those in the "greatest distress may, no doubt, be induced to migrate." Unlike the campaign to the north that the United States fought in the name of protecting "innocent civilians," the southern campaign was largely designed to "prevent the enemy from profiting by the supply of their favorite food which the country affords them." In order to starve the Indians into submission, the United States sent dozens of "boat expedition[s] from Fort Dallas" to destroy "crops and orchards on many a fertile island that the Indians had fondly believed no white man would ever discover." Many of these expeditions went to the "remarkable" area near Fort Dallas called "Arrowroot country." The Seminoles' interest in this area led U.S. General William J. Worth to conclude that "they contended longer for this [area] than for any other stipulation" in their various negotiations. In this manner, the United States hoped to starve the Seminoles into submission.[10]

In the few instances when soldiers tracked down the enemy, they routinely abandoned the rules of warfare designed for European enemies. In December 1840, for example, Lieutenant Colonel William S. Harney led ninety men on one of the most ghastly and widely publicized events of the war. With the assistance of an African American guide named John, Harney's force traveled into the wetlands on sixteen canoes for two days. At Chakaika's island in the Everglades, Harney "dressed and painted his men like Indians" and attacked the village. American soldiers refused the surrender of Chakaika—the leader for whom the island was named—and shot him instead. Harney kept one captured warrior as a guide and ordered a few others to be hanged. Indian family members and loved ones watched as the soldiers executed the condemned warriors and strung up the body of the already deceased Chakaika.[11]

As American soldiers struggled to track down the Native American enemy, they repeatedly faced the prospect of repelling attacks. Seminoles sporadically targeted soldiers as they ventured away from the relative safety of the fort and enjoyed some military successes in their attacks on the Cape Florida lighthouse and other poorly defended coastal outposts. This pattern fits the Seminoles' military tactics, as they rarely initiated assaults on forts but chose to attack when they had the advantage of terrain and surprise. Seminole warriors fired on boats as they made their way up the Miami River and harassed the Fort Dallas soldiers as they marched inland. In a few instances, warriors carefully approached the fort to warn or scare the soldiers. Fighting does not seem to have occurred at the fort, but the fear of attacks created tremendous alarm. On several occasions, the fort was temporarily evacuated, even resulting in some buildings being removed to Fort Bankhead on Key Biscayne in 1838.[12]

These fears ultimately helped convince Fitzpatrick to liquidate his holdings at the North Bank, a process that occurred even as the United States occupied the territory and called it Fort Dallas. In 1841 he mortgaged his Florida lands to his sister, Harriet English, and moved to Texas. He also pursued legal options to recuperate his losses at the North Bank. He placed a claim for losses he incurred as a result of the Indian raids and filed for compensation from the military for illegally occupying his home and confiscating his property. In 1843, while the claims were still pending, the property fell into the hands of Fitzpatrick's nephew, William F. English. The United States government eventually settled the case in 1886, and Congress awarded Fitzpatrick's grandnephew $12,000 for the occupation.[13]

When the Second Seminole War ended in 1842, English tried to reestablish his uncle's plantation. His arrival in south Florida corresponded with the passage of Florida's Armed Occupation Act, which offered free land to settlers willing to defend it from Indians. The arrival of armed settlers brought comfort to English and other white Americans who had purchased or inherited their lands in the midst or on the edges of Indian country. Almost immediately after the United States evacuated Fort Dallas, English "brought a schoonerload of building supplies and a number of slaves, including some who were skilled in construction. He had his slaves occupy the standing buildings and reclear the land and plant limes and lemons, which were still in wide demand for the treatment of scurvy aboard ships." His slaves—some of whom were loaned to him by his mother in Columbia, South Carolina—began to build two additional houses out of limestone: a two-story home to serve as the English family residence and a 97-foot by 17-foot rectangular slave quarters. In addition, English surveyed and laid out a town, tried to sell lots, and dreamed of the riches that would follow. According to one unconvinced observer, English "intends [on] flooding the United States & Key West with Coonti & sugar or whatever else his productive plantation . . . will produce." English's dream went unfulfilled. Rather than promising wealth, the area had little appeal for visitors. One recalled that "I have never in all my travels met with such an immence [sic] number of horseflies & other insects as are to be found here." English may have come to the same conclusion. In 1849, he abandoned his dream of creating a slave plantation to pursue yet another dream. Before the slave quarters were even completed, he went west to join thousands of others on California's Gold Rush. His luck ran out in 1855 or 1856, when he accidentally shot and killed himself as he dismounted from a horse in Grass Valley, California.[14]

With English's departure, the site remained technically deserted for the next few years. As at many other abandoned coastal sites in Florida, squatters occupied the buildings and took advantage of the locale. Their lack of legal ownership did not prevent visitors from describing them as living in settlements. They established a small coontie business to meet the needs of the mostly Seminole clientele. Runaway slaves used the North Bank's coastal access on their attempted escapes to the Caribbean and elsewhere. These activities, which largely occurred outside the gaze of government officials, came to an abrupt halt in 1850 when approximately 150 United States soldiers reoccupied Fort Dallas to deal with "Indian scares." Most of the fears centered on the Fort Myers area to the north and west, but many Americans believed that Billy Bowlegs, Abiaka, and other Seminole leaders occupied camps near the headwaters of the Miami River. Once again the United States used Fort Dallas as a base for soldiers who were able "to march at any moment . . . into the Indian country." These marches led to the capture of a few women before the military abandoned the fort when anxieties about Indian aggressions temporarily abated.[15]

The military would not be gone for long. Almost as soon as it left Fort Dallas, tensions between newly arrived settlers and Seminoles returned. Before the Third Seminole War officially erupted in the region in 1855, the military leased and reoccupied the North Bank, resuming its starvation strategy to "prevent the Indians from visiting the Koontee grounds to procure Koontee, to confine them within their limits, and to prevent all trade with them in violation of the laws of Florida." Once again the location and built environment made the place "the most proper & suitable place for the Military Post that I have seen or can hear of." The site had plenty of lumber, food, fresh water, and buildings that included "a Two Story Stone building, which will answer the purposes of a Storehouse, and the 1st Story wall of a stone building to which I propose to add another story of boards, which when completed will furnish quarters for the two companies."

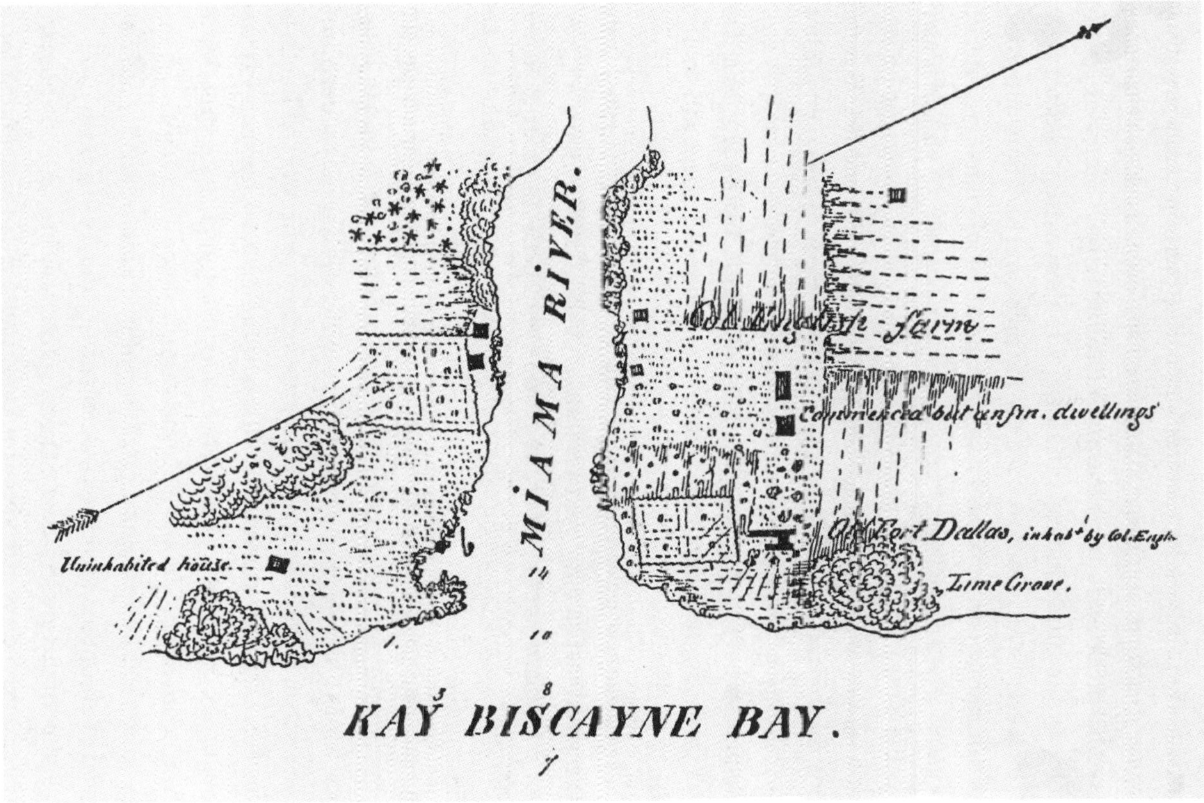

Figure 7. This 1849 map of the "Mouth of the Miama River" details English's landholding, the local mill, the depth of the river's mouth, and an established lime grove. F. H. Gerdes, Map of Fort Dallas, 1849. Printed with permission of HistoryMiami, Florida.

Recent improvements by the military restored the roofs of the stone buildings, but in the absence of white settlers they were "resorted to by the Indians." The Seminoles departed from their temporary home just prior to the military's return. By 1855 the army had already deployed soldiers at Fort Dallas for nearly a year and had begun construction of thirteen new buildings to augment the two preexisting stone structures at the site. They used the oolite rock to reinforce a wall barricade and augment construction materials elsewhere on the site. By the time additional building supplies arrived in April 1855, the military had already opened the barracks and had almost finished the officers' quarters. One soldier recalled that when he arrived with a small group of soldiers after scouting the interior, he was delighted with the respite at Fort Dallas. "Here we saw many nice frame houses among the cocoa palm trees. The ground was high and dry, and the sea breeze was most refreshing after our sojourn through the Everglades. No better place could have been found for a camp." This soldier stayed for only two days, but during the Third Seminole War (1855–1858), these buildings consistently housed about 150 to 180 soldiers.[16]

Fort Dallas's importance to the Third Seminole War resulted from the naval tactics employed to eliminate the Native American presence in the southern part of the Florida peninsula. In order to search the interior systematically, the military constructed a grid of canals and employed a fleet of boats that routinely used the North Bank as a "safe harbor and place of retreat for soldiers." At any one time, the fort housed a small armada. One 1856 account, for example, listed twenty-two different vessels on the premises—one screw boat, one whaleboat, three barges, eight canoes, and ten bateaux. The bustle at the fort increased when the military, under Abner Doubleday's leadership, built a "practicable road" to allow wagons to haul supplies in from Fort Jupiter. Its prime location also made Fort Dallas the announced locale of various diplomatic efforts, none of which materialized or amounted to the removal of the Seminoles.[17]

Most of the soldiers at Fort Dallas stayed only briefly before departing on expeditions to the interior hammocks of dense trees that form islands in the Florida wetlands or to the coastal "Koontee grounds." The list of targeted Seminole villages changed over time, but expeditions repeatedly sought to find and destroy "Waxy Harjo's landing," the New River camp, and Sam Jones's Island. The size of these largely waterborne deployments varied, but most of them consisted of only a few dozen soldiers and a handful of boats. In February 1855, in one of the largest expeditions from the Fort Dallas, the military ordered a "command of about 75 men to cross the Everglades from Miami to Prophets Landing or some other point in the Everglades in its vicinity." When the rather large expedition failed, the soldiers tried again the following month. In March another expedition set off to "explore the route across the Everglades from the Miami river to Prophets Landing, &c." It too failed on account of a drought that made "it impracticable." The inhabitants of Miami, an officer explained, "have never known the water in the Everglades so low as at present at this season." The soldiers found the lack of water a barrier to their travel as it prevented them from skimming across the top of the wetlands in boats. Instead U.S. soldiers tromped through the sawgrass that resulted in "the men suffering very much, from having their feet and limbs cut by the grass."[18]

By protecting and garrisoning Americans who moved into the interior of south Florida, the North Bank's Fort Dallas played an essential role in the expansion of the United States. In early 1856, for example, neighboring Indians attacked settlers in "the neighborhood of Fort Dallas" who had established their homes on Indian lands. Whereas earlier settlements hugged the coast, these homes were "on the border of the Indian hunting grounds, twelve miles west of the fort." Soldiers from Fort Dallas investigated the murders and reported that the two men had been scalped and mutilated. As fear of further reprisals spread, "All of the settlers around the Miami have come into the fort, and demanded the protection of the troops." In the process of explaining the "murder" of the two men, the account dramatically reclassified the wetlands of south Florida. It turned the interior lands that were technically Seminole lands according to various treaties and custom into sovereign U.S. territory.[19]

Even so, American soldiers at Fort Dallas routinely complained about their living conditions. One account in the *Saturday Evening Post* proclaimed: "At Fort Dallas, Florida, mosquitoes are so plentiful that both officers and men rave; the guard on duty pass their whole time under bars." The account continued with even greater hyperbole: "The sentry is provided with a *mosquitto* veil . . . ; woolen clothes, boots, and gauntleted gloves protect the limbs and body from their murderous attacks. Persons who have not experienced the beauty of everglade life will scarcely believe that horses and cattle are actually bled to death in a single night." Wearing protective clothing and burning wet wood kept the mosquitoes at bay, but officers struggled to maintain order in the barracks. This reality manifested itself on March 12, 1857, when Private James Mahoney lashed out at Captain John Milton Brannan. The spark seemed rather minor—Mahoney simply wanted a new "shirt and other articles of clothing" to protect him from the elements and Brannon told him to wait until after the morning's routine roll call. This denial, along with the prospect of going on yet another scout, was too much for Mahoney to bear. He grabbed his musket and attempted to "assault and strike" his captain. At his court-martial, he was found guilty of several counts of disobedience and yet could not escape the monotony of Fort Dallas. In addition to being branded with an "M" on his thigh, the court mandated that he serve two years of hard labor at Fort Dallas. Only the end of the war and evacuation of Fort Dallas in 1858 could provide Mahoney the respite that he desired.[20]

The removal of the Indians to the west or to the "interminable glades" of the Florida interior did not convince the English family to return to their homestead. As in the past, though, it did not remain abandoned for long. As the military evacuated the site, various short-term visitors moved into the formidable site. Its stone and wood buildings remained intact, its gardens and fruit trees flourished, stores of lumber remained, and the soldiers left behind assorted supplies that were not deemed important enough to haul away. Indeed, one woman recalled the general sense of elation when she and other visitors arrived just prior to the evacuation of the fort. In addition to eleven buildings and various tents that housed the soldiers, she remembered that the North Bank was filled with "beautiful coconut trees" and "everywhere was planted in flowers, shrubbery, and vegetables of all kinds. We were provided with all the vegetables that we could make use of fresh from their gardens." These resources and the "unsettled condition" of the North Bank lured dozens of wreckers and others who salvaged what they could from the abandoned military post. Many came from the Bahamas, but others came from the small outposts elsewhere in south Florida. A new community of itinerants slowly transformed the North Bank once again.[21]

The itinerant outpost at the North Bank flourished during the tumultuous American Civil War (1861–1865). No fighting occurred there, and the war remained marginal to the community's daily routines. Even so, the Civil War brought various refugees into a village filled with Bahamians and wreckers from across the American South. As a result, the "motley and villainous-looking crew" included "some twenty or thirty men, of all colors, from the pale Yankee to the ebony Congo, all armed." They included "deserters from the army and navy of both sides, with a mixture of Spaniards and Cubans, outlaws and renegades." Some spoke "broken English." In this manner, the North Bank was an isolated reflection of how the Civil War put virtually all Americans into motion. Men enlisted in armies to march just as others deserted their posts; slaves fled their owners to find freedom behind enemy lines; families moved to find employment or to live with loved ones; and many others became refugees when the enemy forced them out of their homes and laid siege to their towns. The community at the North Bank largely filled with a different set of Americans—men who sought to disappear from the official war. Military deserters, draft dodgers, and blockade-runners (mostly from Florida and the Confederacy more generally) joined the wreckers and others who had taken refuge at the North Bank. Unlike blockade-runners elsewhere, those at the North Bank did not attempt to sneak cotton into the Atlantic marketplace. Instead, they traded with residents from neighboring islands, using items that the North Bank had produced for years—lumber, fish, coontie, and limes. These blockade-runners took shelter there for days or weeks, hoping to avoid detection by naval patrols that periodically secured the Union blockade. Rather than being the home for permanent settlers, the North Bank became the permanent home for dozens of itinerants.[22]

Neither the Union nor the Confederacy felt threatened by the North Bank's community of wartime refugees. It was a small outpost in a state that neither the Union nor the Confederacy saw as essential to the war. Early in the war, some Union officers saw a virtue in occupying the fort in order to get "control of the wreckers," investigate "suspicious looking craft," and obtain access to fresh water and other supplies. Their argument was ignored. The North Bank was too far from the front lines and too marginal to the naval blockade. As a result, neither government allocated the resources needed to reoccupy or otherwise control Fort Dallas. The Union navy occasionally and informally obtained supplies at the North Bank as its ships passed through the bay on their way to Key West or Pensacola, but it relinquished control of the North Bank to self-serving locals. Confederates also worried, albeit halfheartedly, about the North Bank's refugees and the Union's episodic activities there. Confederates, however, largely ignored rumors that the Union was sending woodcutters to the Miami River, just as the Union ignored most reports of Confederate blockade running.[23]

Although the identities of most of the short-term residents have been forgotten, the notable and well-documented experience of John Breckinridge reveals the wartime realities at the North Bank. When the war ended in 1865, the Confederate secretary of war and the rest of the cabinet fled to avoid retribution for their treason. Breckenridge and Secretary of State Judah Benjamin came through Florida, with Benjamin heading to the west coast of Florida and Breckinridge escaping through Fort Dallas. Breckenridge traveled with five others—including John Taylor Wood, the grandson of president Zachary Taylor. Their decision to escape through Biscayne Bay did not come as a surprise. As the Confederates surrendered, U.S. rear admiral Cornelius K. Stribling ordered Union troops to seize Key Biscayne, as "it is not improbable the rebels may try to leave the United States by one of those inlets, as there is a land route to Fort Dallas, at the mouth of the Miami River." Even though Breckinridge got to the bay before the Union could secure it, he and his fellow travelers hesitatingly approached the North Bank. After unsuccessfully scouring the Atlantic shore for food that could be salvaged, the small group decided that they had to "make the venture of stopping at the fort." As Wood explained: "It was running a great risk, for we did not know whom we should find there, whether friend or foe. But without at least four or five days' rations of some kind, it would not be safe to attempt the passage across the Gulf Stream."[24]

Breckenridge and his crew attempted to pass themselves off as fellow "wreckers" to the "hardcase deserters, outlaws, and wreckers" who lived in the "old barracks." Breckenridge refused an offer to land his boat ashore—presumably fearing that they would be captured. Instead, he asked for permission for one of his men to go ashore to trade. A negotiation ensued, and "a canoe paddled by two negroes came off, and said no one but the captain would be permitted to land." Breckenridge refused and threatened to take their "pieces of gold" elsewhere. The refugees at the North Bank would not let them (or their wealth) leave. "Fifteen or twenty men crowded into four or five canoes and dugouts" and pursued Breckenridge's boat. Breckenridge apparently proved that he was a wrecker rather than a military official in the short skirmish that ensued and was allowed to trade. In exchange for gold coins, the Confederate refugees received "a bag of hard bread, two hams, some rusty salt pork, sweet potatoes, fruit [oranges, limes, and bananas], and, most important of all, two breakers of water and a keg of New England rum."[25]

After Breckenridge's escape, most of the other temporary residents returned to their homes or to better opportunities in postwar Florida, the Caribbean, or elsewhere. However, the North Bank and its natural environment remained forever changed by the earlier waves of inhabitants. They left behind the "cocoanut-trees, . . . white buildings," lime trees, freshwater well, and various other items and structures. A small number of Bahamian and American salvagers maintained a presence along the bank, but they no longer formed a permanent community of residents. As a result, the local Indians who visited the community to trade with the "stragglers" at Fort Dallas "discontinued their visits and became distrustful and cautious." The next generation of settlers would choose to erase the memory of these ancient and not so ancient inhabitants. Instead, they would declare themselves to be pioneers, the first real occupants and creators of the community that would become known as Miami.[26]

# Epilogue

## Miami's Pioneers

When the Civil War ended in 1865, a new wave of residents came to the North Bank intent on wrestling civilization from nature. These "first settlers of Miami" ignored or dismissed as failures the centuries of occupants that preceded them and then engaged in acts of physical and intellectual destruction. They allowed some structures to decay, actively razed others, and disregarded the way in which the earlier settlers had physically reshaped the North Bank. They routinely described a property that had been settled for millennia either as in disarray or as an unoccupied and unexploited territory that promised a prosperous future to its prospective owners. They renamed the territory and in the process announced the establishment of the "first" church, courthouse, roads, and settlement. They succeeded because they were "some of the finest men" and "men of ability" and "courage." Within a few decades, these "first" residents of Miami declared the North Bank's two most recent owners to be the city's "mother" and "father." Thousands of years of settlement and occupation served as the backbone of this development, but little more than echoes of the past remained.[1]

The establishment of Miami and the erasure of its long past began almost immediately after the Civil War. With Florida under military rule and carpetbaggers and others hoping to capitalize on the postwar reconstruction of the southern economy, the seemingly unclaimed and unregulated lands of "Tropical Florida" attracted the attention of many investors who hoped to lure immigrants and "new settlers" who could "regenerate & redeem the state." The first of these New South prospectors at the North Bank was William Gleason, Florida's future lieutenant governor. Gleason used his political connections to get a deed to "Swamp lands" at the site, apparently unaware that Harriet English already had a legally binding deed to the property. English defended her title and held onto her investment until 1869, when she sold the property to Dr. Jeptha V. Harris from Key West. The 640-acre property changed hands several times over the next few years, as squatters and others continued to occupy the ancient site.[2]

In 1874, at about the same time that a hurricane came through the region, the Biscayne Bay Company purchased what some deemed to be a "terrestrial paradise [that was] cultivated like the garden of Eden." Most of the postwar visitors were equally impressed with the site. On "the site of old Fort Dallas, two of the buildings . . . still remain standing. What was once the officers' quarters has been transformed into a dwelling-house, and has quite a solid and comfortable appearance, with its thick white walls, wide verandah, and extensive surroundings of shrubbery." Interestingly, the hurricane helped lead others to begin to reimagine south Florida as being in its youth. The strewn trees, broken branches, and general sense of decay that the hurricane inflicted on the North Bank helped subsequent visitors downplay the centuries of occupation and construction that had preceded them. Drawing as much on his experiences in south Florida as from his understanding of the Spanish and British periods, one visitor to the site remarked that "for three centuries and a half, constant changes of nationality and desolating wars have so depopulated and retarded the progress of Florida that she has to-day all the characteristics of a newly settled territory." With these words, a two-thousand-year-old settlement had been labeled the "untamed" frontier.[3]

Typical of the optimism of many investors in the 1870s South and the Gilded Age in general, the Biscayne Bay Company's investors anticipated a quick return on their investment. It hired E. W. Ewan to manage the site, sent him to live in a two-story house originally built by English's slaves, and expected him to transform the dilapidated North Bank into a modern marvel.

Ewan and the company impatiently shifted their investment strategy between promoting the region's "ideal" climate as a "resort for invalids," raising bananas and other "wild" fruits along river, and engaging in the Indian trade. The involvement of the Indian trade, though, was the last resort for a company that imagined itself to be ushering in the modern world. Even as Ewan's control of the property earned him a reputation as the "Duke of Dade [County]," the company's investors and others were disappointed in his efforts to transform the North Bank. Despite his diligent labor, the property reflected its presumed untamed past more than its modern ambitions. Ewan's house stood, as one visitor explained, amid "a great tangle of briars and wild lime trees." Rather than construct something to be envied, Ewan struggled to prevent the site from deteriorating. A year after Ewan's arrival, a visitor declared that only about twenty areas were "cleared and planted with cocoas, guavas, orange and other fruit trees, but now form a wilderness hardly distinguishable from the forest." Alongside the overrun orchards stood "a row of stone-houses, or out-buildings, now falling into ruins." Other descriptions offered similar conclusions about the North Bank's general disrepair and in the process downplayed the enduring elements from its distant and not-so-distant past. "All that remained of Fitzpatrick's slave plantation," one account proclaimed, "were traces . . . in the ruined houses, the grove of cocoa-palms which he planted along the left bank of the Miami river, and the wilderness of fruit trees fast becoming jungle." Despite the lament that the site remained in or was reverting to its natural state, those who were interested could find headstones from Fort Dallas as well as pottery and other ancient items that were unearthed from the local Tequesta mounds.[4]

Ewan ignored the implications that he was building a settlement on top of earlier attempts, but he benefited from the built environment and social connections that had been established generations earlier. Ewan's embrace of the Indian trade resulted from his relation-ship with the owners of the south bank of the Miami River, William and Mary Brickell. The Brickells also purchased their property in 1874 from English, worked as salvagers and fishers, and then estab-lished a trading post for Seminoles and others in the area.

For several years, the Seminoles periodically came to the Miami River to trade various pelts, plumes, and hides for dry goods, metal goods, guns, ammunition, nails, and Singer sewing machines. Ac-cording to one account, "they sell deerskins, buckskin, beeswax, komptie starch, vegetables, bird plumes, alligator teeth, etc., and buy cloth, calico, ammunition, tobacco, etc., and occasionally wy-ho-mee (whisky)." After a brief competition for trade, Ewan and the Brickells combined their efforts. By the end of the 1870s Ewan's efforts had resulted in "Old Fort Dallas" having "a store and a post-office . . . [in] the officers quarters, and offices of the old garrison, which are yet in good condition, being built of stone." In addition, "there are some fine groves of cocoanuts, oranges, lemons, limes, and guavas." Not surprisingly, when boosters for the state of Florida promoted Miami, they pointed to the economic potential of its "tropic and semi-tropical fruits" and the virtues of the "Florida arrow-root, the coontie of the Indians, [that] grows spontaneously upon the rocky lands." Along with trade with the Seminoles, the arrowroot mill at the mouth of the river remained the region's more consistent economic venture. Yet the Brickells would also be marginalized from the public's memory for many years, perhaps because of their connection to the premod-ern Indian trade rather than the modern growth of Miami's history of tourism.[5]

In 1891, Julia Tuttle—who would later earn the unofficial title "Mother of Miami"—purchased the North Bank. A widow from Cleveland, Tuttle originally came to Miami in order to visit her father, Ephraim T. Sturtevant, who had envisioned establishing a coontie empire in the region. Tuttle had different ambitions. Like many be-fore her, she had little interest in maintaining, let alone promoting, the North Bank's ties to the past. She may have moved directly into the living quarters of William English and retained a connection to

Figure 8. Julia Tuttle was widely portrayed as the "Mother of Miami" in the late nineteenth century. Her reputation as a visionary "pioneer" and "founder" remains largely intact today. *Portrait of Julia Tuttle—Miami, Florida* (1890s). Black & white photoprint, 8 × 10 in. Printed with permission of the State Archives of Florida, *Florida Memory*, https://www.floridamemory.com/items/show/29793.

the Indian trade, but she imagined herself as having a transformative role to play. "It may seem strange to you but it is the dream of my life to see this wilderness turned into a prosperous country," Tuttle wrote. One day she hoped to turn "this tangled mass of vine brush, trees and rocks" into "homes with modern improvements surrounded by beautiful grassy lawns, flowers, shrubs and shade trees." Tuttle, along with the Brickells, worked endlessly "to interest people in coming into Dade County, or rather, to Fort Dallas." She invited and hosted dozens of guests at her home with hopes of attracting their assistance in developing the region. These well-heeled visitors learned about the North Bank's storied past, even as they concluded that few of their improvements had any lasting importance. One account declared that with "skillful manipulation," the "plodding homesteader" can attract the "shrill scream of the locomotive . . . where now is seen only the sail-boat and the Indian canoe."[6]

Another guest, James Henry Ingraham, came to a similar conclusion. Ingraham, the president of the South Florida Railroad Company of the Plant System, concluded that Tuttle had "shown a great deal of energy and enterprise in this frontier country where it is almost a matter of creation to accomplish so much in so short a time." She "converted [the fort] into a dwelling house after being renovated and repaired with the addition of a kitchen, etc. The barracks . . . is used as office and sleeping rooms." Despite Tuttle's "improvement . . . on hammock land which fringes the river and bay," Ingraham explained, the natural world remained largely untamed. "Lemon and lime trees," which were planted by the earlier waves of Spanish, Bahamian, and American occupants, "are growing wild all through the uncleared hammock."[7]

Tuttle's boosterism fit within the attitudes of a larger community of recently settled Miamians who declared themselves to be "pioneers" near the end of the nineteenth century. As newcomers established homesteads across south Florida, they portrayed their acts as "courageous" attempts to tame the frontier. One 1891 account declared that "Dade County is in the main inaccessible to ordinary tourists and unopened to the average settler. [It] is inhabited only by the remnants of the Seminole Indians, and is visited only by the more enterprising and adventurous of hunters and cowboys." Tuttle herself diminished the efforts of the earlier white inhabitants, who admitted to trying only halfheartedly to transform the region. One lazy neighbor, she claimed, tried to "plant something," but concluded that it was not worth it because "there don't seem much to come of it." Despite Tuttle's pronouncements that the pioneers began a new history at the North Bank, their behavior did not deviate very far from that of many of the earlier inhabitants of the North Bank. They worked as wreckers, dreamed of connecting their community to the southern and Atlantic economies, and otherwise saw the mouth of the Miami River as the center of their community.[8]

Tuttle gained her reputation for "founding" Miami via her role in Henry Flagler's decision to extend the East Coast Railroad from Palm Beach to Miami at the end of the nineteenth century. White neighbors and later historians would elevate Tuttle for bringing a new vision to the site. In 1952, for example, Florida senator Scott M. Loftin decried "astute and far-sighted business men as John Egan, Richard Fitzpatrick, William F. English, Dr. J. V. Harris and members of the Biscayne Bay Company" for failing "to realize that they held the site of a future city in their hands." With 20/20 hindsight, the senator added that "it remained for a wise and remarkable woman to envision its possibilities."[9]

Tuttle spent much of the early 1890s trying to lure Flagler and other railroad builders to Miami. The railroad symbolized modernization—both in its physical and mechanized imagery and in its potential to transform locations that were otherwise distant from civilization. Railroads allowed "palace cars from Bar Harbour and Newport," Maine, to "roll unimpeded through the poverty-littered Carolinas" and into Florida. In the winter of 1894–1895, most of Florida suffered from a series of freezes. On December 24, 1894, and December 28, 1894, freezing temperatures devastated the orange crop in north and central Florida. When another freeze hit in February 6, 1895, other agricultural interests were affected as well. Although Flagler had already decided to extend the railroad south to Miami, Tuttle sent him a gift of orange blossoms to show him that the freeze had not reached the "isolated locality" in the southern peninsula. Flagler announced the extension of the railroad shortly thereafter. Tuttle, however, offered Flagler more than orange blossoms. Flagler also received some of Tuttle's North Bank property in order to build a luxury hotel. Even the name of the establishment, the Royal Palm Hotel, drew attention to the newly planted royal palm trees at the site—trees that were imported from Cuba and neighboring Caribbean islands.[10]

Building the hotel in 1895 and 1896 required workers to transform mangroves and wilderness into graded property and a grid of streets. The primarily African American laborers broke axes on ironwood trees, struggled to get tree roots out of coral rocks, and suffered from the poisonous saps of local trees and vines. What backbreaking labor could not achieve, dynamite ultimately did. At the end of the nineteenth century, progress and technology went hand-in-hand with Jim Crow segregationist norms. Indeed, twelve African Americans lived in tents on the site before they began construction of the hotel. These individuals, despite the presence of hundreds of earlier black occupants, are widely seen as Miami's first black residents. In addition to these workers, Flagler relied heavily on convict laborers who were paid $2.50 a month to work on the extension of the railroad. Once construction began, these black workers formed Colored Town to the northwest of the river, an area later incorporated as Overtown.[11]

Constructing the hotel and its magnificent grounds required these and other construction workers to bury the earlier history of Miami. They demolished many of the natural features of the site, parts of Fort Dallas, and many of the other building on premises. The destruction of the ancient mounds and Indian presence had begun years earlier, but Flagler's men brought a new zeal to the effort. When the construction began, a large burial mound still "stood out like a small mountain, twenty to twenty-five feet above water" and "about one hundred feet long and seventy feet wide." The burial mound and other physical reminders of the past were seen as roadblocks to the newly incorporated Miami's future rather than as windows to its past. Flagler's African American workers struggled to remove "a poison tree" that grew on the top of the mound, as it "would knock them cold." Without much debate, those workers "who were not allergic to it" leveled the mound, uncovering and hastily removing "between fifty and sixty skulls." The midden materials from the mound were strewn across the property, while other smaller mounds faced similar destruction. One of the workers took home the bones: he "stored them away in barrels and gave away a great many . . . to anyone that wanted them." When construction ended, he dumped the remaining skeletons "nearby where there was a big hole in the ground." The location of the site, "near Second Street & Second Avenue," would later become the home of John W. Watson. Even the workers noticed that they were doing more than burying history: "There is a fine residence now standing over the bones—and the things that the owners don't know will never hurt them."[12]

The construction workers were equal opportunity destroyers of the past—removing many of the physical reminders of the Spaniards, Seminoles, United States military, and English as well as the free and enslaved black inhabitants who lived there previously. When the laborers uncovered "a beautiful gold crucifix, evidently belonging to a Catholic priest" from the Spanish era, they gave "this wonderful find" to Joseph A. McDonald, the supervisor of the construction site. Workers also "found a great many skeletons, lots of items which may have belonged to soldiers stationed at Ft. Dallas." The "grading of the grounds" led to the removal of a three-foot by four-foot "wooden headstone" that marked "the grave of a soldier [named Granger] who died at Fort Dallas in . . . 1837." In addition they found, and kept, "handmade metal canteens, odds and ends of pottery jars—glass beads and other objects." Other items—including a gold earring and various beads—were deposited shortly after in Loxahatchee Historical Museum in Jupiter, Florida. Construction and destruction went hand in hand, with the birth of a "new" Miami erasing the physical reminders of the old.[13]

Even the 1896 decision to name the new city "Miami" largely ignored the history of the river's North Bank. Although it had been known as "Tequesta," "Fitzpatrick's Estate," "Fort Dallas," and

"Biscayne Bay Country," few white residents considered those names to be appropriate for their new city. When city founders first created a city charter in 1896, some proposed naming it after Flagler. Flagler, however, insisted on naming the town after the Miami River. In the name-choosing process, the city "founders" effectively erased the ancient and not-so-ancient past. They left the impression that "in its adolescent days . . . we had all come from somewhere else." Without an acknowledged past, "history still had to be scribbled": Miami could become "the city that Flagler built" and Tuttle could become the "Mother of Miami."[14]

When the Royal Palm Hotel opened on January 1897, promoters billed it as the birthplace of Miami. The idea stuck. In the decades that followed, Flagler and others reduced Miami's past to that of "a little Indian trading post." One early history declared that "there were only two families living in Miami" in 1895. A historical overview of the city written when Miami was "only 1 year old" began the story with the establishment of Fort Dallas, described as little more than "a temporary station" that was quickly "abandoned." Another declared that the "ruins of the old fort" were "still standing," before describing the wild "beauty" and natural "abundance" at the site. A half century later, in 1954, F. Page Wilson typified the public's understanding of Miami's history by explaining that "when the Flagler railroad was built to a spot in the jungle on the Miami river known sometimes as Fort Dallas or sometimes Miami, this became the nucleus or starting point for the entire region." John Sewell, a foreman for Henry Flagler, buttressed this myth when he announced after Miami's incorporation that when he had arrived a couple of years earlier he "found Miami all woods."[15]

Although diminished in its importance, Fort Dallas served as the city's prehistory. For several years, Miami's "pioneers" used the memory and namesake of Fort Dallas to sell themselves as "founders." These boosters imagined themselves to be engaged in a militaristic task akin to that of the hardy English colonists of earlier times and the homesteaders of the West. Tuttle's otherwise converted and luxurious home retained its militarized identity as Fort Dallas's barracks; a bank and other institutions borrowed Fort Dallas's name; and guides for tourists routinely began with Fort Dallas's place in the city's prehistory. Miami's nostalgia for its military past served an important function, which was repeated elsewhere. The United States routinely described pioneers as white Americans who first settled the lands after it ceased to be the frontier—a euphemism that in the late nineteenth century meant that place where "civilization met savagery." Subduing the Indian, as indicated by the end of the Third Seminole War, allowed for progress and history to begin in south Florida. Settlers, in essence, were portrayed as the first inhabitants to occupy an area after the elimination of the Native American presence. This perspective continued through the twentieth century, leading historians to spread the pioneers' version of history. As one historian explained: "Founded as an army outpost on the northern banks of the river which bore its name, Miami's genesis was also the result of the Seminole Wars." In short, the privileging of Fort Dallas allowed Americans to forget the area's Indian and Spanish pasts and allowed the Seminole Wars to initiate Miami's history. Much like León and the Spanish "discoverers," the boosters who first promoted Miami drew upon ideas about progress and modernity that allowed them to ignore inconvenient truths about the past.[16]

For nearly three decades, the Royal Palm Hotel stood as a symbol of the extravagant future of south Florida. The Royal Palm Hotel cost more than $750,000 to build, an astronomical sum at the time. It stood five stories tall with a sixth-floor salon and offered luxurious accommodations to as many as 600 guests at a time. Its ballroom, which was filled to its 500-person capacity on opening night, offered a lavish dining menu that included turtle soup, baked pompano, quail, and broiled filet of beef. Flagler also built a dock and had the mouth of the river and the bay dredged in order to accommodate shallow-draft steamships that could help transport supplies and hotel guests to New York and the Bahamas. Although episodic memories of the past remained—largely related to the large "cocoanut trees on the old Fort Dallas grounds . . . that are fully 80 feet high"—most

Figure 9. Flagler's Royal Palm Hotel attracted guests from around the country, while its park served as a local and public meeting place for many events on Miami's growing social calendar. *Bird's Eye View of the Royal Palm Hotel and Park—Miami, Florida* (1922). Black & white photoprint, 8 × 10 in. Courtesy of the State Archives of Florida, *Florida Memory,* https://www.floridamemory.com/items/show/41057.

visitors marveled at the contrast between the hotel and its frontier-like surroundings.[17]

The erasure of the North Bank's early history continued after the construction of the hotel. Visitors to the site frequently understated its past in order to exaggerate the real transformations that occurred in south Florida. Indeed, Miami was changed from a rural to an urban community relatively quickly. Miami's white population skyrocketed to over 100,000 only a few years after the construction of the Royal Palm Hotel. The new city increasingly became a destination for midwestern and northeastern white tourists. The forgetting of the prepioneer past also occurred in the form of nostalgia. One visitor from Au Sable Forks, New York, declared that "after an absence of some thirty-five years" he returned to the North Bank to find "the change in Miami greater than any he has known."[18] This sentiment was repeatedly echoed elsewhere, as writers marveled at the city's emergence from a "small frontier town to a metropolitan community" or from a "wilderness into thriving town." Another self-declared pioneer explained that he grew up when "the south end of the state was just emerging from its raw pioneer days." This history began as a "small settlement at the mouth of the river . . . [when] a few pioneers had settled in the area." By the time the history was told later, writers had dismissed the possibility of there being lasting vestiges of the past. An undated "brief history of Fort Dallas" from the early twentieth century, for example, began its history with William English.[19]

In time, even Fort Dallas stood in the way of the North Bank's future. In this context, historical preservationists played a significant role in helping erase Miami's ancient history. Often working with the false belief that General Francis Dade built Fort Dallas, members of Miami's Women's Club and Everglades Chapter of the Daughters of the American Revolution (DAR) raised money to move the barracks off of its original site to nearby Lummis Park. Dade was a Second Seminole War leader who never visited south Florida and was killed at the outset of the war, but his name became the moniker of Miami's county in his martyrdom. Nonetheless, after several years of fundraising, the building was moved in 1925, when it became the

DAR headquarters. The "oldest building" in the city became known for its connection to the wars of origin for both the United States and Florida.[20] The timing of the move was equally telling. As construction workers moved the historic structure, city "founders" held an annual "Pioneers' day" in order to recall the "days of no streets, no electricity, no water with the exception of pumps, plenty of mosquitoes, sand flies, and other insects."[21] By the late twentieth century Dade County's Historic Preservation Division could imagine its history as stretching *From Wilderness to Metropolis* between 1825 and 1940. Only echoes remained of the history that predated Fort Dallas.[22]

Shortly after the barracks were moved, in October 1926, a powerful hurricane left much of Miami in shambles. Many boats were left high and dry and hundreds of buildings were damaged; the Royal Palm Hotel fared worse than most. The hotel and most of its auxiliary buildings were immediately deemed uninhabitable, and souvenir hunters salvaged what they could from the site. As its owners debated the desirability and expense of fixing and reopening the hotel, the October 1929 stock market crash ended any redevelopment plans. In June 1930 the dilapidated Royal Palm Hotel was demolished. A decade later, developers removed the "last relic of Miami's early history"—an eight-foot wall built out of coral rock when the North Bank was known as Fort Dallas during the Seminole Wars. It was "removed to make space for a garage where 1940 automobiles will be sold."[23]

The ultimate razing of the human improvements on the North Bank resulted in the loss of memory about the peoples and the generations of environmental alterations that occurred on the site. In due time, a paved parking lot replaced the coontie plants, "wild" lime and coconut trees, well, and stone walls. Memories and statues of white Gilded Age founders would overshadow the memory of Miami's earlier settlers—the Tequestas, enslaved Africans, Bahamians, white planters, wreckers, Seminoles, refugees, and soldiers. By the time of the North Bank's destruction and erasure from the public memory, the city that it spawned would continue to grow in size and importance. Although its specific role would be reduced, the North Bank

Figure 10. The officers' quarters at Fort Dallas remained a public symbol of Miami's transformation from military outpost to tourist town. This widely printed image displays the domestication of the military's past. *Fort Dallas Quarters Turned into a Home—Miami, Florida* (ca. 1900). Black & white photoprint, 8 × 10 in. Courtesy of the State Archives of Florida, *Florida Memory*, https://www.floridamemory.com/items/show/38001.

remained at the geographic center of the modern city of Miami. This site was Miami's birthplace, and only now are its residents beginning to reimagine their ancient pasts.

St. Augustine typically receives accolades for being the oldest continuously occupied city in the United States. Despite their valiant efforts, Florida scholars and boosters have largely failed to dismantle Jamestown's or Plymouth's place in the American imagination. Americans conceive of their "origins"—as the durability of the Pocahontas and Thanksgiving stories attest—as being outside of the Spanish world. In many ways, Michael Gannon's lament that "by the time the Pilgrims came ashore at Plymouth, St. Augustine was up for urban renewal" remains true.[24] However, it too inadvertently obscures the pre-Spanish history of Florida and the United States more generally. By the time the Spanish founded St. Augustine in 1565, Miami had already gone through many rounds of urban renewal of its own. With its first visitors arriving 3,500–4,000 years ago and a permanent settlement forming at least 2,000 years ago, Miami's long history dwarfs that of the city widely known as "America's oldest." To be fair, Miami is not the oldest continuously settled city in North America either. Many, if not all, of the colonial towns that fill history books and tourist guides originally began as Indian towns. These memories, however, have long been forgotten. In the quest to establish "firsts" and establish European origins, scholars and civic boosters have erased countless ancient and indigenous histories. As a result, the voices and perspectives of settlers and pioneers drown out those of the original inhabitants. This volume seeks to help continue the process of remembering these forgotten ancient histories for Miami, Florida, and elsewhere.

# Acknowledgments

M Y PARENTS AND GRANDPARENTS migrated to south Florida decades after the destruction of the Royal Palm Hotel. The Franks
and Kleins were all born in New York but lived much of their adult
lives on reclaimed Florida lands. They were settlers in their own way,
occupying lands that once flowed like a river of grass and housed
Seminoles and their ancestors. In Florida, my family lived in new
bedroom communities and helped found and build various voluntary
organizations. My earliest memory of my Florida home is the ocean
of imported white sand that covered my plotted but yet-to-be-built
neighborhood. Like many, we imagined that our town's founders settled the region in the 1920s after drainage created a grid of canals and
farms. Years later, I married into the Tendrich and Seitlin families,
whose ties to Miami extend further back to the early twentieth century. They proudly tell stories of settling and pioneering, of establishing civic and religious institutions, and of a small-town Miami that
hardly matches my more modern image. Their stories contain local
rowboats competing against newly arrived steamships on the Miami
River, repeated land grabs, and Jim Crow segregation and religious
intolerance. Their stories are like many of the publicly repeated tales
in south Florida; they largely ignore more ancient stories in favor of
the struggles of starting society afresh. I may have attended Seminole
Middle School and grew up amid local Tequesta mounds, but a huge

gap separated Native American history from my own. These older stories were not unknown, but they were practically untold.

*Before the Pioneers* joins a larger academic and civic community of studies that have been trying to reclaim south Florida's ancient past. In doing so, I have relied on the work of many scholars who have preceded me and on a community of colleagues and friends who have aided and abetted my journey. As a result, my intellectual and personal debts are many. In particular, I would like to extend my sincere gratitude to various archaeologists who helped guide this work. This list includes Daniel Seinfeld, Jeff Ransom, Robert Carr, Glen Doran, Mary Glowacki, Hank Kratt, and various members of the Panhandle Archaeological Society of Tallahassee, Florida Division of Historical Resources, and Seminole Tribe of Florida Tribal Historic Preservation Office. I reserve special thanks for Jerry Milanich, who served as one of my outside readers and graciously improved the manuscript with his insights. Sian Hunter, at the University Press of Florida, provided tremendous guidance throughout the researching and writing of this book. I could not have asked for a better editor.

For their assistance in researching this project, several archivists and scholars deserve special praise. Dawn Hugh and the rest of the staff at HistoryMiami Museum helped track down manuscripts and otherwise guide me through their priceless (and unfortunately un- derappreciated) archive. Paul George graciously welcomed me to the museum's collections and to the history of Miami, even as I encoun- tered the intellectual footprints that he established over his distin- guished career. Arva Parks, whose own unpublished work on the site proved invaluable, similarly read the entire manuscript and offered invaluable insights into the history and manuscript. Like all histori- ans of Florida, I owe additional debts to Jim Cusick and the rest of the staff at the P. K. Yonge Library at the University of Florida, who of- fered invaluable assistance. I also owe similar debts to staff members (past and present) at Florida State University's Library and Special Collections, including William Mudrow, who provided unparalleled assistance at the project's infancy. Finally, Christopher Crenshaw, Tif- fany Hensley, and James Hendry Miller all deserve special gratitude.

They worked tirelessly in a rather short span of time to help gather, cull, and sort many of the research materials for the project.

I am privileged to have many generous and supportive colleagues at Florida State University, and I relied heavily on Jennifer Koslow and Frederick Davis for their guidance and an additional cup of coffee when needed. Ed Gray provided me with intellectual support early in the project and encouraged me to use my expertise in this fashion. The Department of History and College of Arts and Sciences provided me with time, a precious resource, to complete this project. Elsewhere, Kristopher Ray provided advice at critical stages, especially when his distance from Miami and Florida studies was needed. I would also like to express my sincere appreciation to a group of historians and archaeologists at the University of Miami who patiently heard and discussed an early draft of this project. They forced me to embrace the implications of development in Miami's past and in its present. In particular, Michael Bernath and Karl Gunther graciously hosted me, and Traci Ardren and Will Pestle offered articulate and honest skepticism about my historical interpretation and the modern development of the property. They pushed me toward a better and different final product.

Eugene Stearns deserves a special note of appreciation for his involvement during the earliest stages of this project. My interest in it began with a phone call from him in February 2014. A distinguished trial lawyer and FSU alum, Stearns represented the developer who was engaged in dispute with historical preservationists and others about the future of a plot of land on Miami River's North Bank. He wanted to know as much history as he could about the Miami property, and after a 15-minute phone call I did as well. I hope that my early research (as incomplete as it was) helped lead his client to preserve and interpret more of the site and destroy less of it. I own Stearns gratitude for trusting my interpretations and insisting from the outset that I maintain my intellectual independence.

Finally, my family has been a source of endless support and love. My parents, Paul and Judie Frank, have provided me with a lifetime of limitless love and have supported my journey into academia even as it was filled with uncertainties. They instilled in me a love for learning at a very young age and remain as committed as ever to the virtues of a liberal arts education. My brother, Gary, has been a constant source of stability and friendship and has heard more about this project than he bargained for. I am also humbled that my in-laws, Howard and Marilyn Tendrich, have embraced me and connected me to many of the people and places of old and new Miami. Long before I started this project and as I worked on it, Grandma Helen Tendrich and Grandpa Jack and Grandma Shirley Seitlin similarly shared countless stories about Miami's past. I hope that they would recognize the Miami in this book. My three children, Daniel, Noah, and Shayna, inspire me to see old things afresh, as if I am seeing them again for the first time. Their hugs and smiles are my sustenance. Without Lisa Tendrich Frank this project could not have been completed. She has read every word of this book more than once and heard me rant about every detail and discovery at least a dozen times. For twenty plus years, she has been my partner in everything we do. She is my copilot in life, my best friend, and a tremendous historian. I love her everything and for everything.

# Abbreviations

| | |
|---|---|
| AGI | Archivo General de los Indios, Seville, Spain, microfilm at PKY |
| *ASPIA* | *American State Papers, Indian Affairs.* 2 vols. Washington, DC: Gales and Seaton, 1832–1834 |
| *ASPPL* | *American State Papers, Public Lands.* 8 vols. Washington, DC: Gales and Seaton, 1832–1861 |
| CP | Chadron Papers, HM |
| EFP | East Florida Papers, LC, microfilm at PKY |
| *FA* | *Florida Anthropologist* |
| *FHQ* | *Florida Historical Quarterly* |
| FM | Floridamemory.com, online repository of the State Archive of Florida, Tallahassee |
| HM | HistoryMiami Museum, Miami, Florida |
| LOC | Library of Congress, Washington DC |
| LR | Letters Received |
| LROAG | Letters Received by the Office of the Adjutant General (Main Series) 1822–1860, M-564, NARA |
| LS | Letters Sent |

M1084 Letters Sent, Registers Of Letters Received, and Letters Received by Headquarters, Troops in Florida, and Headquarters, Department Of Florida, 1850–1858, Microcopy 1084, NARA

NARA National Archives, Washington, DC

NMCCF Records Relating to Navy Marine Corps Coast of Florida

OHT Oral History Transcripts, HM

OR *The War of the Rebellion: A Compilation of the Official Records of the Union and Confederate Armies.* Washington, DC: Government Printing Office, 1880–1901

PKY P. K. Yonge Library, University of Florida, Gainesville

PR Returns from Military Posts, 1800–1916, Microcopy 617, reel 284, NARA

PRO Public Records Office

RG 45 Records Relating to the Service of the Navy and Marine Corps on the Florida Coast during the Florida War, December 29, 1835–August 14, 1842, Record Group 45, NARA

RG 393 Letters Sent by the Department of Florida and Successor Commands, April 18, 1861–January 1869, Record Group 393, NARA

SLG Spanish Land Grants, FM

TFP Tuttle Family Papers, HM

TP Clarence Edwin Carter, ed., *The Territorial Papers of the United States.* Washington, DC: Government Printing Office, 1934–

# NOTES

INTRODUCTION: MIAMI'S LOST HISTORY

1. Many scholars have attempted to connect the ancient and modern worlds in Florida and the United States more generally. For a few recent attempts, see Calloway, *One Vast Winter Count*; Ethridge, *From Chicaza to Chickasaw*; and Richter, *Before the Revolution*. Throughout this volume, I have retained the original spellings in quotations.

2. Parks, "History of Coconut Grove," 2; Portes and Stepick, *City on the Edge*, 61.

3. Pittman and Waite, *Paving Paradise*.

4. Milanich, *Florida Indians and the Invasion from Europe*, 52–53.

5. Judd, *Second Nature*; Reilly, *Tropical Surge*, 90. See Cronon, *Nature's Metropolis*, xix; Poole, *Saving Florida*, 136–137; Bert Collier, "Miami Could Mean 'Sweet Water' Again," *Miami News*, October 5, 1961; Charles Powell and Lawrence Mahoney, "Sweet Water," *Tropic Magazine* (March 15, 1970): 25–30.

6. Milanich, *Laboring in the Fields of the Lord*; Kropp, *Adobe Vieja*.

7. Mormino, *Land of Sunshine*; Stepick et al., *This Land Is Our Land*, 39; Portes and Stepick, *City on the Edge*, 208.

8. Mormino, "So Many Residents, So Few Floridians"; Davenport, "Growing Up, Sort of, in Miami," 11. See Reed, "South But Not Southern."

9. Whitfield, "Florida's Fudged Identity"; Gannon, *Florida*, 4; Belleville, *Salvaging the Real Florida*. Modern scholars and Seminoles are both pushing

back on the notion that the Seminoles were "colonies" that broke off from the Creeks. For a discussion of the connections between ancient Floridians and modern Seminoles, see Wickman, *Tree That Bends*; Frank, "Creating a Seminole Enemy"; Jackson, "Seminole Histories of the Calusa."

10. There are some exceptions, as both Miami and the North Bank have been blessed with diligent academic and popular historians who have not received enough attention. Two of the most active scholars have both written works that focus on the Miami River as well as volumes and articles about topics that span the city's history. See Parks, *Where the River Found the Bay*; George, *Along the Miami River*.

11. Rainbolt, *Town That Climate Built*, 15. See Roberts, *Gone Sunwards*, 11–12, 110–111, 164–177. Julia Tuttle's contribution to the development of Miami, like those of women in general in American history, came as an afterthought. See Ione Stuessy Wright to Howard Kleinberg, August 3, 1985, *Miami News*, Miami Pioneer Papers, Correspondence; Ida M. Vihlen letter to editor, clipping from *Miami Daily News*, May 11, 1934, Vihlen Family Papers, HM. Ironically, this redress of a historical oversight resulted in the magnification of another. In this case, the rush to crown Tuttle as the mother of Miami resulted in the overlooking of Mary Brickell, who had a similar role in attracting moneyed interests in the late nineteenth century. See Joanne Cavanaugh, "A Slight Made Right," clipping in Miami Pioneers, Inc. Papers, Box 13, HM.

12. Richter, *Before the Revolution*, 4. See Andrew Viglucci, "Tequesta Archaeological Find in Downtown Miami Is Boon to Historians," *Miami Herald*, February 8, 2014.

13. Carr, *Digging Miami*, xiii. See Frances Robles, "Miami's Past and Future Clash at Building Site," *New York Times* (May 19, 2014).

## Chapter 1. Before the North Bank

1. Harper, "Agricultural Conditions in Florida in 1925," 349.

2. Purdy, *Florida's People during the Last Ice Age*, 1; Zeiller, *Prehistory of South Florida*, 9–16.

3. Randazzo and Jones, *Geology of Florida*; Hoffmeister, *Land from the Sea*, 19–26.

4. Meltzer, *First Peoples in a New World*, 183–208.

5. Purdy, *Florida's People during the Last Ice Age*, 44.

6. Wentz and Gifford, "Florida's Deep Past," 330–337.

7. Clauser, "Archaeological Excavations at Ichetucknee Springs"; Hemmings, "Paleoindian and Early Archaic Tools of Sloth Hole."

8. Purdy et al., "Earliest Art in the Americas," 2908–2913; Meltzer, *First Peoples in a New World*, 80, 82, 89.

9. McGoun, *Ancient Miamians*, 6–17; Carr, *Digging Miami*, 27–45; Carr, "Early Man in South Florida," 62–63; Wheeler, *Southern Florida Sites Associated with the Tequesta and Their Ancestors*.

10. Milanich, *Florida Indians and the Invasion from Europe*, 19–20.

11. Krech, *Ecological Indian*, 29–43; Milanich, *Archaeology of Precolumbian Florida*, 61–69.

12. Milanich, *Archaeology of Precolumbian Florida*, 61–69.

13. Doran, *Windover*; Milanich, *Archaeology of Precolumbian Florida*, 70–75.

14. Wentz, "Origins of American Medicine"; Wentz, *Life and Death at Windover*; Doran, *Windover*.

15. McGoun, *Prehistoric Peoples of South Florida*, 54; Milanich, *Florida Indians and the Invasion from Europe*, 37–62.

16. Milanich, *Archaeology of Precolumbian Florida*, 70.

17. Zeiller, *Prehistory of South Florida*, 12; Myers and Ewel, *Ecosystems of Florida*.

18. Hoffmeister, *Land from the Sea*, 28. See McGoun, *Prehistoric Peoples of South Florida*, 12; McCally, *Everglades*, 37–38.

19. Carr, *Digging Miami*. See the reports of Robert Carr, John Mann Goggin, and Shawn Bonath, in Master Site File, 8DA00011; Bonath, "Archaeological Research Strategy for the Granada Site."

## Chapter 2. The Founders

1. Griffin et al., *Excavations at the Granada Site*, 365–394. See Master Site File, 8DA00011. Ecologists and environmental historians use the term "second nature" to distinguish landscapes that have been modified and shaped by their interaction with human population from those more pristine untouched lands. Judd, *Second Nature*.

2. McGoun, *Prehistoric Peoples of South Florida*, 99. See Hann, *Indians of Central and South Florida*, 141; Milanich, *Hernando de Soto*, 114–117; Master Site File, 8DA00011.

3. Griffin et al., *Excavations at the Granada Site*, 149; Carr et al., "Phase II Archaeological Survey," 3–4; Wheeler, "Southern Florida Sites," 55–56; Carr, *Digging Miami*, 103–142.

4. Milanich, *Florida Indians*, 112; Wheeler, *Southern Florida Sites*, 4; McCally, *Everglades*, 10–16.

5. Fontaneda, *Fontaneda's Memoir*, 13. See Nellis, *Poisonous Plants and Animals of Florida and the Caribbean*, 29, 162; Smith, "Ethnological and Archaeological Significance of Zamia," 240–242.

6. Griffin, *Archaeology of the Everglades*, 123–160, 290; Sturtevant, "Last of the South Florida Aborigines"; Goggin, "Archaeology of the Glades Area," 69.

7. Goggin, "Cultural Traditions in Florida Prehistory," 28–29. See Griffin et al., *Excavations at the Granada Site*, 1:365–366.

8. Lewis, *Neither Wolf Nor Dog*, 9; Goggin, "Tekesta Indians of South Florida."

9. Scarry, "Paleoethnobotany of the Granada Site"; Larson, *Aboriginal Subsistence Technology*, 223, 227; Goggin, "Tekesta Indians of Southern Florida," 283; Masson and Scarry, "Carbonized Seeds and Corn Cobs from the Honey Hill Site (8DA411)"; Scarry and Newsom, "Archaeobotanical Research in the Calusa Heartland," 395; Goggin and Sturtevant, "Calusa," 180, 184–185, 188; Purdy, *Art and Archaeology of Florida's Wetlands*, 236.

10. Bawaya, "Amazing Tale of the Miami Circle"; Widmer, "Archaeological Investigations at the Brickell Point Site, 8DA12," 57; Carr, *Digging Miami*, 232–248; Wheeler, "Archaeology of Brickell Point and the Miami Circle"; Billie, "Miami Circle and Beyond"; Dixon et al., "Provenance of Stone Celts"; Wheeler and Carr, "It's Ceremonial, Right?" Although the veracity of the astronomic argument is not very strong, public discussions of the site routinely refer to this as an equally valid interpretation. For example, Levin, *Liquid Land*, 188.

11. Dixon et al., "Provenance of Stone Celts," 328.

12. Shea, "Ancient Florida," 274.

13. Wenhold, *17th Century Letter*, 11.

14. Velasco in Swanton, *Early History of the Creek Indians and Their Neighbors*, 389; Milanich, *Florida Indians and the Invasion from Europe*, 123.

15. Parks, *Where the River Found the Bay*, 142. See Hann, *Indians of Central and South Florida*, 142; Milanich, *Florida Indians and the Invasion from Europe*, 52–53; Carr, *Digging Miami*, 106–110; Carr et al., *An Archaeological*

*Survey of Southeast Broward County,* 24–25; Wheeler, "Archaeology of Brickell Point and the Miami Circle."

16. Wheeler et al., "Archaic Period Canoes from Newnans Lake, Florida"; Vollaro, "Sixty Indians and Twenty Canoes," 136; Hann, "Tequesta Sources Translation," 3.

17. Carr and Reiger, "Strombus Celt Caches in Southeast Florida"; Griffin, *Archaeology of the Everglades,* 308; Luer, "Calusa Canals in Southwestern Florida"; Luer and Wheeler, "How the Pine Island Canal Worked"; Wheeler, "Naples Canal."

18. Goggin, "Tekesta Indians of Southern Florida"; Hann, *Missions to the Calusa,* 220; Lewis, "Calusa," 27, 29; Goggin and Sturtevant, "Calusa," 187–189; Merás, *Pedro Menéndez de Avilés,* 210, 222. See Widmer, *Evolution of the Calusa,* 82, 88.

19. Kolianos and Weisman, *Florida Journals of Frank Hamilton Cushing,* 113–118.

20. Lowery, *Spanish Settlements,* 64.

21. Kenny, *Romance of the Floridas,* 337.

22. Adair, *History of the American Indians,* 134.

23. Hann, *Missions to the Calusa,* 319.

24. Bullen, *Florida Indians of Past and Present,* 333.

25. Goggin, "Tekesta Indians of Southern Florida," 282. See Wallace, "Native American Tattooing in the Protohistoric Southeast."

## Chapter 3. Spanish Colonialism and the Doctrine of Discovery

1. Herrera y Tordesilla, *Historia general,* 248. See Peck, "Reconstruction and Analysis of the 1513 Discovery Voyage"; Kelly, "Juan Ponce de Leon's Discovery of Florida," 54, 57–58; Milanich and Milanich, "Revisiting the Freducci Map"; Milanich, "Charting Juan Ponce de León's 1513 Voyage to Florida"; Fuson, *Juan Ponce de León and the Discovery of Puerto Rico and Florida.*

2. Davis, "Juan Ponce de Leon's First Voyage," 16, 17, also 39–40, 49. See Kelly, "Juan Ponce de Leon's Discovery of Florida"; Keegan, *People Who Discovered Columbus,* 207, 216, 222–223; Fuson, *Juan Ponce de León and the Discovery of Puerto Rico and Florida,* 85–88.

3. Miller et al., *Discovering Indigenous Lands,* 4, 9–13, 55, 69; Miller, "Doctrine of Discovery," 87–91.

4. Fontaneda, *Fontaneda's Memoir*, 47. See Weber, *Spanish Frontier in North America*, 32–33; Vega, *Florida of the Inca*, 10–18.

5. Crosby, *Columbian Exchange*; Kelton, *Epidemics and Enslavement*, esp. 51–82; Worth, "Razing Florida."

6. Hoffman, "Until the Land Was Understood," 71; Laudonnière, *Three Voyages*, 68; Menéndez in Connor, *Colonial Records of Spanish Florida*, 1:35. See McCally, *Everglades*, 40.

7. Fontaneda, *Fontaneda's Memoir*, 27–28. See Bushnell, "Ruling 'the Republic of Indians.'"

8. Arrate y Acosta, *Llave del Nuevo Mundo*; Hann, *Missions to the Calusa*, 420; Fontaneda, *Fontaneda's Memoir*, 29.

9. Hann, *Missions to the Calusa*, 303. See Lowery, *Spanish Settlements*, 260.

10. Pedro Menéndez de Avilés to the King, October 20, 1566, AGI, 54-1-31/176. See Barrientos, *Pedro Menéndez de Avilés*, 222.

11. Hann, *Missions to the Calusa*, 280, 299–300. See Swanson, *Documentation of the Indians*, 9; Ribas, *My Life among the Savage Indians*, 249–251; Zubillaga, *Monumenta Antiquae Floridae*, 31.

12. Hann, *Missions to the Calusa*, 220, 309. See Hann, *Indians of Central and South Florida*, 141; Milanich, *Timucua*, 89; Milanich, *Laboring in the Fields of the Lord*, 93–97; Ruidíaz y Caravia, *La Florida*, clxxxvi.

13. Merás, *Pedro Menéndez de Avilés*, 229–232; Villareal to Rogel, January 23, 1568, in Hann, "Tequesta Sources Translation," 1. See Ugarte, "First Jesuit Missions in Florida," 75–79; Parks, "Where the River Found the Bay, 33. See Lewis, "Calusa," 28; Wilmeth and Bigsby, *Cambridge History of American Theater*, 1:22. Parks received essential (and since then largely ignored) assistance from historian Eugene Lyons, who translated the earliest Spanish records about colonial Florida.

14. Zubillaga, *Monumenta*, 235–240. See McNicoll, "Caloosa Village Tequesta," 15; Swanson, *Documentation of the Indians*, 10; Hoffman, *Florida's Frontiers*, 55; Hoffman, *Spanish Crown*, 142–143; Ugarte, *Los mártires de la Florida*, 29–32.

15. Zubillaga, *Monumenta*, 235–240. See McNicoll, "Caloosa Village Tequesta," 15; Hann, "Tequesta Sources Translation," 5.

16. Zubillaga, *Monumenta*, 235–240. See Alegre, *Historia de la provincia*, 1:62; Certification of Capt. Pedro Reynoso of items received in the presidios

of Carlos, Tequesta, and Tobaga, exclusive of foods supplies in Havana, June 23, 1569, AGI, CD942, No. 5.

17. Zubillaga, *Monumenta*, 321, 416. See Connor, *Colonial Records of Spanish Florida*, 1:73–75; Swanson, *Documentation of the Indians*, 11; Hann, *Missions to the Calusa*, 263, 220; Alegre, *Historia de la provincia*, 65.

18. Zubillaga, *Monumenta*, 361, 372–373; Hann, *Missions to the Calusa*, 263, 309.

19. Velasco, *Geografía*, 86.

20. Wenhold, *17th Century Letter*, 11–12; Goggin, "Tekesta Indians," 277.

21. Brooks, *Unwritten History of St. Augustine*, 75. See Ribas, *My Life among the Savage Indians*, 249; Carballido y Zúñiga, *Chronological History of the Continent of Florida*, 161.

22. Hahn, *Missions to the Calusa*, 314. See Milanich, *Florida Indians and the Invasion from Europe*, 53; Hoffman, *Florida's Frontiers*, 53; True, "Some Early Maps Relating to Florida," esp. 83; True, "Freducci Map of 1514–1515."

23. Sauer, *Sixteenth Century North America*, 191; Lyon, *Enterprise of Florida*, 166; Pedro Menéndez to Crown, October 20, 1566, AGI Santo Domingo, 168; Fuente, *Havana and the Atlantic*, 45–46.

24. Connor, *Colonial Records of Spanish Florida*, 1:33, 47, also 103–105. See Lyon, *Enterprise of Florida*, 148–149; Parks, *Where the River Found the Bay*, 28; Hann, *Missions to the Calusa*, 8.

25. Connor, *Colonial Records of Spanish Florida*, 1:31, 33, 35, 37, 39, 41, 135 See Hann, *Missions to the Calusa*, 302; Pedro Menéndez de Avilés to the King, October 20, 1566, Stetson Collection, PKY; Weber, *Spanish Frontier in North America*, 56–57.

26. Connor, *Colonial Records of Spanish Florida*, 33, 35, 37, 41; Bishop Gerónimo Valdís of Cuba to the Crown, December 9, 1711, AGI, 58–2-10/1; Governor of Cuba to the King, July 26, 1743, AGI 58–2-10/13; Governor of Cuba to the King, July 7, 1732, AGI 58–2-10/4; Governor to King, July 26, 1743, AGI 58–2-10/13; Bishop Geronimo Valdés of Cuba to the Crown, December 9, 1711, AGI 58–2-10/1; Gallay, *Indian Slave Trade*, 295.

27. Crane, *Southern Frontier*, 81; Braund, "Creek Indians, Blacks, and Slavery," 606. See Adair, *History of the American Indians*, 134.

28. Hann, *Missions to the Calusa*, 420.

29. Childers, "Life in Miami and the Keys," 59–60. See Weber, *Spanish Frontier in North America*, 72; Hann, *Missions to the Calusa*, 420; Swanson,

*Documentation,* 39 and fn187; Hann, "Summary Guide to Spanish Florida Missions," 428; Lyon, *Enterprise of Florida,* 201–203.

30. Roberts, *An Account of the First Discovery,* 19; Juan José Elisio de la Puente to the Governor of Havana, December 12, 1764, AGI 87–1-5; Davies, *Calendar of State Papers,* 106. See Report of the Mission, September 28, 174, CP.

31. Fernán de Martínez, Map of Florida, 1765, AGI 86-5-24; Adair, *History of the American Indians,* 134; Romans, *Concise Natural History of East and West Florida,* 29, 296. See Sturtevant, "Last of the South Florida Aborigines"; Sturtevant, "Chakaika and the Spanish Indians"; Worth, "Razing Florida"; Worth, "Creolization in Southwest Florida"; Worth, "Tracking the Calusa Overseas."

## Chapter 4. Gateway to the Caribbean

1. This episode does not appear in the main historical studies of Bowles. See Wright, *William Augustus Bowles,* 55–70; Narrett, *Adventurism and Empire,* 215–228, 254–255, 259–261.

2. Murdoch, "Documents concerning a Voyage."

3. Wright, *William Augustus Bowles,* esp. 62-72. See Frank, *Creeks and Southerners,* 40, 44, 113.

4. Vicente Manuel de Zespedes to Domingo Cavello, March 12, 1790, EFP, PKY, reel 8 section 2; Thomas Forbes to John Leslie, August 10, 1791, EFP, PKY.

5. Murdoch, "Documents concerning a Voyage," 28.

6. Chardon, "Northern Biscayne Bay in 1776," esp. 37. For an exception, see Parks, *Where the River Found the Bay.*

7. Riordan, "Finding Freedom in Florida."

8. Ellicott, *Journal of Andrew Ellicott,* 252.

9. Larry Smith, "Coconut Grove: Bahamian Roots in Florida," *Nassau Tribune,* October 12, 1977; Muir cited in Reilly, *Tropical Surge,* 41. See Saunders, *Bahamian Loyalists and Their Slaves,* 1–17; Ledin, "Tropical and Subtropical Fruits in Florida," 350; *Niles Register,* November 15, 1817; Mohl, "Black Immigrants," 271.

10. De Brahm, *Atlantic Pilot,* 15; Aikin, *Geographical Delineations,* 372; *Georgia Gazette,* October 7, 1790; Hammond, "Wreckers and Wrecking."

11. Governor of Florida to Sec. of Grace and Justice Antonio Porlier (draft), December 10, 1790, EFP, PKY, reel 15, doc 3; Ellicott, *Journal of*

*Andrew Ellicott*, 252. See Hoffman, *Florida's Frontiers*, 413; Blank, *Key Biscayne*, 19, 27.

12. Wickman, *Tree That Bends*; Frank, "Creating a Seminole Enemy"; Jackson, "Seminole Histories."

13. Covington, "Trade Relations between Southwestern Florida and Cuba."

14. Kersey and Bannan, "Patchwork and Politics," 197; Martin, Field Notes; Small, "Seminole Bread," 121.

15. Waselkov and Braund, *William Bartram*, 59–62; MacCauley, *Seminole Indians of Florida*, 484; Kersey, "Havana Connection"; McNeill, "Sailing Vessels of the Florida Seminole."

16. Vignoles, *Observations upon the Floridas*, 134; Porter, "Negroes and the Seminole War," 278; Forbes, *Sketches, Historical and Topographical*, 105. See Howard, "'Wild Indians' of Andros Island," 280–281.

17. *Bahama Herald*, November 9, 1853. See *Bahama Herald*, November 24, 1853; *Bahama Herald*, December 21, 1853; *Bahama Advertiser*, October 2, 1819; Kersey, "Seminole Negroes," 170; Howard, *Black Seminoles in the Bahamas*; Porter, "Notes on Seminole Negroes."

18. Hoffer, *Law and People in Colonial America*, 25–26.

19. Romans, *Concise Natural History*, 263, 288, 265; De Brahm, *Report of the General Survey*, 241–242. See Waselkov and Braund, *William Bartram*, 259–260; Chardon, "Cape Florida Society of 1773"; De Brahm, "Hydrogeographical Map of the Southernmost Part of East Florida."

20. De Brahm, *Atlantic Pilot*, 11; Romans, *Concise Natural History*, 260.

21. Siebert, *Loyalists in East Florida*, 2:53; Waselkov and Braund, *William Bartram*, 49; Romans, *Concise Natural History*, 263. See Beeson, *Fromajadas and Indigo*, 26.

22. Frazier, "Samuel Touchett's Florida Plantation"; Schafer, "Early Plantation Development," 42; Bailyn, *Voyagers to the West*, 465–466; Roberts, *Account of the First Discovery*, 521; Juan Nepomuceno de Quesada to Luis de las Casas (draft), November 15, 1794, EFP, PKY, reel 9, section 2; Juan Xavier de Arrambide to Ayuntamiento (document obliterated), February 1, 1814, EFP, PKY, reel 175, section 99.

23. Frank, "Taking the State Out."

## Chapter 5. Becoming Southern

1. Baptist, *Creating an Old South*, 20–21; Black, "Richard Fitzpatrick's South Florida, Part I" and "Richard Fitzpatrick's South Florida, Part II."

2. Schafer, *William Bartram*, 29–38; Weber, *Spanish Frontier*, 297–300.

3. Burkhardt, "Starch Making," 47–49; Sturtevant, "Chakaika and the Spanish Indians," 37–43.

4. Reilly, *Tropical Surge*, 41; James Hagen [Hagan] Land Grant, SLG, https://www.floridamemory.com/items/show/232689; *ASPPL* 4: 422, 572, 596; "True Cope of a Certificate and Opinion of Title to the Mrs. Hagan (or Rebecca Egan) Donation"; "East Florida," *Niles Weekly Register* (November 15, 1817): 189.

5. Johnson, *Bahamas: from Slavery to Servitude*, xiv.

6. Siebert, *Legacy of the American Revolution*, 7–10; Hamilton, "Spanish Land Grants in Florida"; Parker, "Men without God or King"; Poitrineau, "Demography and the Political Destiny of Florida."

7. *Spanish Land Grants in Florida*, 3:207–208; Bonawit, *Miami, Florida Early Families, and Records*. See James Hagen [Hagan] Land Grant.

8. McDonough, *Francis Richard Family*, 56; Marotti, *Cana Sanctuary*, 30, 56. See Cusick, *Other War of 1812*, 1–12.

9. Hammond, "Dr. Strobel Reports on Southeast Florida," 69.

10. Brown, *Florida's Peace River Frontier*, 25, 28.

11. James Hagen [Hagan] Land Grant; Susan Hagen [Hagan] Land Grant, SLG, https://www.floridamemory.com/items/show/232690; *ASPPL*, 422, 572, 596; Hudson, "Beginnings of Dade County," 27; Cash, "Lower East Coast," 58–59.

12. *Key West Register and Commercial Advertiser*, February 19, 1829. See Black, "Richard Fitzpatrick's South Florida, Part II," 35.

13. Williams, *Territory of Florida*, 50, 78.

14. Black, "Richard Fitzpatrick's South Florida, Part I," 48, also 34, 35, 37, 40. See Cash, "Lower East Coast," 59, 71 n10; Hudson, "Beginnings of Dade County," 28; Shapee, "Fort Dallas and the Naval Depot," 31.

15. Black, "Richard Fitzpatrick's South Florida, Part I," 50.

16. William Hasell in *Pensacola Gazette*, May 2, 1828; Denham, *"Rogue's Paradise,"* 12.

17. Black, "Richard Fitzpatrick's South Florida, Part I," 60, also 52–54, 59–60. See Stebbins, *City of Intrigue*, 8–19.

18. Forbes, *Sketches, Historical and Topographical*, 118.

19. Baptist, *Half Has Never Been Told*, 18, also 86. See Johnson, *River of Dark Dreams*, 13, 45.

20. Black, "Richard Fitzpatrick's South Florida, Part I," 48, 55. See Hudson, "Beginnings of Dade County," 13–14; Shapee, "Fort Dallas and the Naval Depot," 32.

21. Baptist, *Half Has Never Been Told*, 115, also 115–120. See Shapee, "Fort Dallas and the Naval Depot," 31.

22. Black, "Richard Fitzpatrick's South Florida, Part II," 40. See Baptist, *Creating an Old South*, 49; extract from the report of Gerdes to Supt. Bache, 1850, CP.

23. Black, "Richard Fitzpatrick's South Florida, Part II," 50, also 35, 38–39. See *Journal of the Proceedings of the Legislative Council*, 99, 108; Wolfe and Wolfe, *Names and Abstracts*, 42.

24. Kirk, "William Cooley," 16, Dodd, *Florida Becomes a State*, 293.

25. Black, "Richard Fitzpatrick's South Florida, Part II," 43. See Hudson, "Beginnings of Dade County," 13–14; Shapee, "Fort Dallas and the Naval Depot," 32.

## Chapter 6. The Armed Occupation of Fort Dallas

1. Kirk, "William Cooley"; *TP*, 26:417, 485; Black, "Richard Fitzpatrick's South Florida, Part II," 36, 39–41; W. A. Whitehead to Stephen Pleasanton, October 3, 1835, CP; *TP*, 25:325; Rose Wagner Richards, "Reminiscences of the Early Days of Miami," CP.

2. Mahon, *History of the Second Seminole War*; Kappler, *Indian Affairs*, 344–345, 394–395.

3. *Reports of the Courts of Claims*, 2. See W. A. Whitehead to Stephen Pleasanton, October 3, 1835, CP; A. C. Richards, "Early Days on New River, Miami River, and Biscayne Bay," August 8, 1905, 26, CP; Brown, "Race Relations in Territorial Florida," 304 n75; Mahon, *History of the Second Seminole War*.

4. Kirk, "William Cooley," 17; *TP*, 26:417, 485; Frank, *Creeks and Southerners*, 35–40.

5. Kirk, "William Cooley," 17; *TP*, 25:246–247; Mahon, *History of the Second Seminole War*; Motte, *Journey into Wilderness*, 223–224, 309.

6. *Causes of Hostilities of Seminole Indians*, 19–20; "Florida War," *Niles Weekly Register* (February 15, 1840); "The Bloodhounds," *Liberator* (March 20, 1840); "Indian Murders in Florida: The Truth of History," *Army and*

*Navy Chronicle* (February 20, 1840); "The Bloodhounds," *Army and Navy Chronicle* (February 20, 1840). See *Tallahassee Star*, January 9, 1840; Campbell, "Seminoles."

7. McLendon, *Pioneer in the Florida Keys*, 30; Hoole, *Florida Territory in 1844*, 37; Munroe, *Through Swamp and Glade*, 317; Coffman, *Old Army*, 116–117; Doubleday, "Military [Auto]Biography of Certain Chapters." See *Historical Fort Dallas*, 2.

8. J. K. Paulding to I. Mayo, June 14, 1839, NMCCF, roll 197; Zachary Taylor to Roger Jones, March 24, 1839, NMCCF, roll 197; Paulding to Mayo, December 2, 1839, NMCCF, roll 197; James Gadsden to Lewis Cass, December 4, 1833, in *Seminole Hostilities*, 130. See Shapee, "Fort Dallas and the Naval Depot," 13, 24, 27, and 28; Taylor to Mayo, July 16, 1838, NMCCF, roll 197; PR, March 1839; TP, 25:227.

9. PR, October 1839; Martin Burkam to Thomas Childs, October 5, 1841, NMCCF, roll 260; Burkam to Childs, November 5, 1841, NMCCF; roll 260; Munroe, *Through Swamp and Glade*, 328; J. H. Baldwin, May 25, 1840, NMCCF, roll 202; Mayo to Sec. of the Navy, July 25, 1839, NMCCF, roll 260; Buker, "Mosquito Fleet's Guides," 313. The monthly post returns repeatedly reveal the trouble with military discipline at the site, as they listed soldiers "under arrest" or "in confinement." See PR, February 1838, February 1840, October 1841.

10. Gadsden to Cass, December 4, 1833, in *Seminole Hostilities*, 130; *Causes of Hostilities of Seminole Indians*, 19–20; Hoole, *Florida Territory in 1844*, 27; J. W. Gunnison to Taylor, May 4, 1839, NMCCF, roll 197; Fitzpatrick to Call, 1836, in *Proceedings of the Military Court of Inquiry in the Case of Maj. Gen. Scott*, 294–206. See also PR, December 1841.

11. Mahon, *History of the Second Seminole War*, 283–284. See Harney to William W. S. Bliss, December 24, 1840, NMCCF, roll 197, 202; Sturtevant, "Chakaika and the Spanish Indians," 51–54; Reavis, *Life and Military Service of Gen. William Selby Harney*, 144–145; Burkam to Childs, October 5, 1841, LROAG, roll 260; Mayo to Sec. of Navy, July 30, 1839, RG 45.

12. TP, 25:324–325; PR, March 1839; "Correspondence of Commercial Advertiser," *New York Spectator* (April 26, 1838); Taylor to Jones, March 9, 1839, NMCCF, roll 197; "Domestic Intelligence: Florida War," *Army and Navy Chronicle* (July 16, 1840); "Domestic Intelligence: Florida War," *Army and Navy Chronicle* (March 28, 1839); C. E. Woodruff, letter, *Army and Navy*

*Chronicle* (May 2, 1839); "The Late Capt. S. L. Russell, U.S.A.," *Army and Navy Chronicle* (March 28, 1839).

13. Black, "Richard Fitzpatrick's South Florida, Part I," 62–63; Shapee, "Fort Dallas and the Naval Depot," 30–34; *Claim of Richard Fitzpatrick*.

14. Douglas, *Everglades*, 254; Hoole, *Florida Territory in 1844*, 37. See *Historical Fort Dallas*, 9; "True Copy of a Certificate and Opinion of Title to the Mrs. Hagan (or Rebecca Egan) Donation," 3, CP.

15. F. H. Gerdes to A. D. Bache, February 5, 1949, CP; Childs to W. W. Mackall, November 19, 1850, M1084, 1:79–80. See Report of Gerdes to Supt. Bache, 1850, CP. See Marotti, *Heaven's Soldiers*, 84; Eck, "South Florida's Prelude to War," 75–76; PR, October 1849–December 1850, reel 284; Rivers, *Rebels and Runaways*, 79–80, 108.

16. Haines to Bennett H. Hill, December 11, 1854, M1084, roll 1:66; Hill to John Munroe, January 13, 1855, M1084, roll 4; Munroe to S. Cooper, December 26, 1855, M1084, roll 1: 174; Hill to Haines, April 18, 1855, M1084, roll 4; Canova, *Life and Adventures in South Florida*, 44. See Haines, Memorandum, December 11, 1854, M1084, roll 4; "The Military Posts in South Florida," *Daily Picayune* (April 8, 1856); Shapee, "Fort Dallas and the Naval Depot"; *Historical Fort Dallas*, 2.

17. Haines to Hill, April 20, 1855, M1084, roll 1:109; Doubleday, "Military [Auto]Biography of Certain Chapters." See Haines to Haskin, February 19, 1855, M1084, roll 1:87; Francis N. Page, December 14, 1856, List of Boats, Barges &c, 1856, M1084, roll 5; Wickman, "A 'Trifling Affair.'" See the routes to Ft. Lauderdale and the Everglades in *Military Map of the Peninsula of Florida*; Ives, *Memoir to Accompany a Military Map*.

18. Hill to Thomas M. Vincent, January 20, 1856, M1084, roll 4; Harris to Hill, February 19, 1855, M1084, roll 1:88; Hill to Haines, March 10, 1855, M1084, roll 4; Hill to Morris, January 1, 1856, M1084, roll 4; Hill to Vincent, January 12, 1856, M1084, roll 4; Munroe to Cooper, August 15 1855, M1084, roll 1:137; Instructions to Cap. [Samuel K.] Dawson for exploration through the Everglades, June 11, 1855, M1084, roll 4. See Bell to Hill, September 23, 1856, M1084, roll 5; Dawson to Hill, March 9, 1855, M1084, roll 4; "The Florida Indians," *Daily Globe* (June 22, 1857); Canova, *Life and Adventures in South Florida*, 65.

19. "Our Key West Correspondence," *Weekly Herald* (February 2, 1856); "Indian Murders in Florida," *Daily Pioneer and Democrat* (April 18, 1856).

20. "A Delightful Country," *Saturday Evening Post* (August 22, 1857); Mahoney Court Martial, May 13, 1857, Records of the Office of the Judge Advocate General (Army), RG 153, HH783, NARA.

21. Williams, *Territory of Florida*, 143; Richards, "Reminiscences of the Early Days of Miami," 9, CP. See Shapee, "Fort Dallas and the Naval Depot," 32; Dillon, "South Florida in 1860," 446; Dodd, "Wrecking Business," 185–186; Nordhoff, "Wrecking on the Florida Keys," 584.

22. Wood, "Escape of General Breckenridge," 318. See Charles Howe to J. H. Spotts, December 4, 1861, *OR*, Ser. 1, 16:799–800; W. C. Molloy to Gideon Welles, January 8, 1863, *OR*, Ser. 1, vol. 17: 346; John Milton to Jefferson Davis, October 5, 1863, in *Letters of Jefferson Davis*, 10; Wynne and Crankshaw, *Florida Civil War Blockades*, 34, 35, 62, 113, 118, 127; Dillon, "Gang of Pirates"; Sternhell, *Routes to War*, 113–118, 140–151; Richards, "Early Days on New River," 39–40, 46–59, CP.

23. Second report of conference for the consideration of measures for effectually blockading the coast bordering on the Gulf of Mexico, September 3, 1861, *OR*, Ser. 1, vol. 16:652. See W. C. Molloy to Gideon Welles, January 8, 1863, *OR*, Ser. 1, vol. 17:346.

24. Report of Acting Rear-Admiral Stribling, U.S. Navy, regarding measures for the capture of President Davis and Cabinet, May 3, 1865, *OR*, Ser. 1, vol. 17: 838; Wood, "Escape of General Breckenridge," 317.

25. Wood, "Escape of General Breckenridge," 317; Hanna, "Escape of the Confederate Secretary of War."

26. Wood, "Escape of General Breckenridge," 317; John T. Sprague to George S. Hartstuff, January 19, 1867, RG 393.

### Epilogue: Miami's Pioneers

1. Interview with Helen Budge Wright, January 21, 1971, OHT; Hill, "Recollections of Early Miami," 5; *First Thirty Years of Miami*, 15. See O'Brien, *Firsting and Lasting*; interview with Russell Pancoast, February 3, 1966, OHT; Wolfe, "Settler Colonialism," 387–409.

2. Pozzetta, "Foreign Colonies in South Florida," 47–51; James F. B. Marshall in Clark, "Florida, 'Our Own Italy,'" 58. See Harris Family Indenture, 1870, 1874, HM.

3. Buck, "Biscayne Sketches at the Far South," 78; Townshend, *Wild Life in Florida*, 236–238. See Shapee, "Fort Dallas and the Naval Depot."

4. *Biscayne Bay*, 3, 18; Parks, "Miami in 1876," 112; George, "Passage

to the New Eden," 442; Day, "Trip to Miami"; Blackman, *Miami and Dade County*, 18; Excerpts from the Florida diary of Andrew E. Douglas, January 23, 1884, HM; "English Sportsman in Florida: Third Paper," *Appleton's Journal of Literature, Science and Art*, March 13, 1875; Townshend, *Wild Life in Florida*, 236–238. See Perrine, *Biscayne Bay*, 13; Wilson, *Miami*, 25–27; Sewell, *Memoirs and History of Miami*.

5. Cited in Sturtevant, "Seminole Personal Document," 58; J. A. Henshall, "A Winter in East Florida," *Field and Stream* (November 20, 1879); Robinson, *Resources and Natural Advantages of Florida*, 12, 108. See Marchman, "Ingraham Everglades Exploring Expedition," 28; Martin, *Florida's Flagler*, 151; Carr, "Brickell Store"; Kersey, *Pelts, Plumes, and Hides*, 30; Hudson, "Beginnings of Dade County," 31.

6. Muir, *Miami U.S.A.*, 49; Dorn, "Recollections of Early Miami," 45–46; "Subtropical Florida," *Scribner's Magazine* 3 (March 1894): 362; Mrs. E. T. Sturtevant, *The Semi-Tropical: A Monthly Periodical Devoted to Southern Agriculture, Horticulture, Immigration, Etc.*, edited by Harrison Reed (2 vols.; Jacksonville: Charles Blew, 1876), 2:205.

7. Marchman, "Ingraham Everglades Exploring Expedition," 29. See Tuttle, "Life in Dade County," 204; Martin, *Florida's Flagler*, 152; Akin, *Flagler*; Brickell, *William and Mary Brickell*, 76.

8. Norton, *Handbook of Florida*, 19; M. Arter, "Sunlit, Sea-Kissed Miami," *Miami News*, March 29, 1901. See George, "Passage to the New Eden"; Mormino, *Land of Sunshine*; interview with Maude Richards Black, April 17, 1969, OHT; interview with Joseph Cheetham, July 29, 1953, OHT.

9. Carson, "Miami," 6.

10. Woodward, *Origins of the New South*, 297; Martin, *Florida's Flagler*, 153. See Parks, *Miami*, 63–81; Allman, *Miami*, 120–122; Standiford, *Last Train to Paradise*, 65; Carson, "Miami"; Flagler to Tuttle, August 24, 1896, TFP.

11. Martin, *Florida's Flagler*, 153; Parks, *Where the River Found the Bay*, 142; Standiford, *Last Train to Paradise*, 66.

12. Parks, *Where the River Found the Bay*, 142; *Historical Fort Dallas*, 11; Connolly, *World More Concrete*, 20–21; interview with Jack Sewell [1970s], OHT. Modern archaeologists bemoan the spreading of the midden and mound materials, as their destruction has irrevocably complicated the reconstruction and analysis of the ancient communities that occupied the area.

13. Straight, "Early Miami," 67–68.

14. Revels, *Sunshine Paradise*, 48–49; Wright, *More Than Petticoats*, 19; Peters, *Miami*, 26.

15. *Golden Days*, 29; *First Thirty Years of Miami*, 3; Norton, *Handbook of Florida*, 311; *Historical Fort Dallas*, 2, 6; Arva Moore Parks in *Miami Centennial Ball*, 1, HM; Wilson, "Miami," 27; Rose Wagner Richards, "Reminiscences of the Early Days of Miami," DP. See *Florida Facts for Tourists*, 23; interview with Hattie Carpenter, March 1953.

16. *Florida*, 25; George, "Passage to the New Eden," 442.

17. H. W. van Deman, "Fruits in Southern Florida," *Colman's Rural World*, April 16, 1914. See *First Thirty Years of Miami*, 14; Benjamin Hammond, "The Tropical Laboratory at Miami and Some Other Things," *American Gardener* (May 3, 1902): 288. Simpson, *Ornamental Gardening in Florida*, 139; "Miami, Fla.," *American Florist* 15 (December 2, 1899): 527; George, "Passage to the New Eden," 445; Stephens, "Port of Miami," 3.

18. Fort Dallas Register, March 22, 1901, Miami, Florida, HM.

19. Cox Family History, HM 1, 4; [1943] clipping, Stoneman Scrapbook, HM; "Brief History of Fort Dallas," HM.

20. "Women to Raise Fund for Moving Old Fort Dallas," *Miami News* (March 31, 1925); "Fund for Moving Old Fort Dallas Climbs to $3000," *Miami News* (April 8, 1925); "Save Old Fort Dallas," *Miami News* (May 18, 1923); "A Brief History of Fort Dallas," HM.

21. Clipping from *Miami Daily News*, May 11, 1934, in Vihlen Family Papers, HM.

22. Metropolitan Dade County Office of Community Development, *From Wilderness to Metropolis: The History and Architecture of Dade County (1825–1940)*.

23. "Ancient Miami Coral Rock Wall to Be Torn Down," *Victoria Advocate* (January 7, 1940). See *Pictorial History of the Florida Hurricane*, 8; Laxon, "Dupont Plaza Site," 55.

24. Gannon, *Florida: A Short History*, 4.

# BIBLIOGRAPHY

## Unpublished Sources

"A Brief History of Fort Dallas." Typescript. HM.

Clauser, John W. "Archaeological Excavations at Ichetucknee Springs, Suwannee County, Florida." Report Number 10 (December 1973), PKY.

Cox Family History, HM.

Day, Joseph H. "A Trip to Miami, 1877." Typescript. HM.

De Brahm, John William Gerard. "Hydrogeographical Map of the Southernmost Part of East Florida" (1771). Geography and Map Division, LOC.

Doubleday, Abner. "Military [Auto]Biography of Certain Chapters, 1846–1858." MS 1987–211, New York Historical Society, Microfilm, HM.

Excerpts from the Florida diary of Andrew E. Douglas and related letters, 1883–1960, HM.

Goggin, John Mann. "The Archaeology of the Glades Area, Southern Florida." PKY.

Hagen [Hagan], James. Land Grant. Florida Memory, State Library and Archives of Florida, http://www.floridamemory.com/items/show/232689.

Hagen [Hagan], Susan, Land Grant, Florida Memory, State Library and Archives of Florida, http://www.floridamemory.com/items/show/232690.

Hann. John H. "Tequesta Sources Translation: First Spanish Period." HM.

Harris Family Indenture, 1870, 1874, HM.

Hill, Allen T. "Recollections of Early Miami." HM.

Letters Sent by the Department of Florida and Successor Commands, April 18, 1861–January 1869, RG393, NARA.

Mahoney Court Martial, May 13, 1857, Records of the Office of the Judge Advocate General (Army), RG 153, HH783, NARA.

Martin, Jack. Field Notes, 2011. http://mvskokecountry.wordpress. com/2011/06/01/field-notes-jack-martin-2011.

Master Site File, 8DA00011. Tallahassee, FL: Bureau of Archaeological Research, Division of Historical Resources, Florida Department of State.

Member of F Company, 2nd U.S. Artillery Regiment. "Untitled View of Fort Dallas, at the Outlet of the Miami River into Biscayne Bay" [Fort Dallas, Florida, 1849–50], http://bostonraremaps.com/inventory/the-first-view-of-miami-florida.

Miami Pioneers, Inc. Papers. HM.

Office of the First Auditor, Records of the Accounting Officers of the Department of the Treasury. RG 217, NARA.

Returns from U.S. Military Posts, 1806–1916. M1083, reel 284, NARA.

Stetson Collection, PKY.

Stoneman, Frank. Scrapbook, HM.

"True Cope of a Certificate and Opinion of Title to the Mrs. Hagan (or Rebecca Egan) Donation." Florida State University Special Collections.

Vihlen Family Papers, HM.

**Books and Articles**

Adair, James. The History of the American Indians. Edited by Kathryn E. Holland Braund. Tuscaloosa: University of Alabama Press, 2009.

Aikin, John. Geographical Delineations: Or, a Compendious View of the Natural and Political State of All Parts of the Globe. Philadelphia: F. Nichols, 1807.

Akin, Edward N. Flagler: Rockefeller Partner and Florida Baron. Kent, Ohio: Kent State University Press, 1988.

Alegre, Francisco Javier. Historia de la provincia de la Compañia de Jesús de Nueva España. 3 vols. Rome: Institutum Historicum, 1960.

Allman, T. D. Miami: City of the Future. Gainesville: University Press of Florida, 2013.

American State Papers: Documents of the Congress of the United States in Relation to the Public Lands, from the First Session of the Eighteenth to the Second Session of Nineteenth Congress, Inclusive: Commencing December 1, 1823, and Ending March 3, 1827. Washington, DC: Gales and Seaton, 1859.

Arrate y Acosta, José Martín Féliz de. *Llave del nuevo mundo: Antemural de las Indias Occidentales, La Habana descripta: Noticias de su fundación, aumentos y estados.* Havana, Cuba: Comisión Nacional Cubana de la UNESCO, 1964.

Bailyn, Bernard. *Voyagers to the West: A Passage in the Peopling of America on the Eve of the Revolution.* New York: Knopf, 1986.

Baptist, Edward E. *Creating an Old South: Middle Florida's Plantation Frontier before the Civil War.* Chapel Hill: University of North Carolina Press, 2002.

———. *The Half Has Never Been Told: Slavery and the Making of America Capitalism.* New York: Basic Books, 2014.

Barrientos, Bartolomé. *Pedro Menéndez de Avilés: Founder of Florida.* Translated with an introduction by Anthony Kerrigan. Gainesville: University Press of Florida, 1965.

Bawaya, Michael. "The Amazing Tale of the Miami Circle." *American Archaeology* 6, no. 2 (2002): 12–19.

Beeson, Kenneth Henry. *Fromajadas and Indigo: The Minorcan Colony in Florida.* New York: History Press, 2006.

Belleville, Bill. *Salvaging the Real Florida: Lost and Found in the State of Dreams.* Gainesville: University Press of Florida, 2011.

Beuker, George E. *Blockaders, Refugees, and Contrabands: Civil War on Florida's Gulf Coast, 1861–1865.* Tuscaloosa: University of Alabama Press, 2004.

*A Bill for the Relief of Richard Fitzpatrick.* U.S. House of Representatives. Bill 616, 33rd Congress, 2nd Session, January 5, 1855.

Billie, Bobby C. "The Miami Circle and Beyond." *St. Thomas Law Review* 13 (2000): 113–115.

*Biscayne Bay, Dade Co., Florida, between the 25th and 26th Degrees of Latitude: A Complete Manual of Information concerning the Climate, Soil, Products, etc., of the Lands Bordering Biscayne Bay in Florida.* Albany: Weed, Parsons and Company, 1876.

Black, Hugo L., III. "Richard Fitzpatrick's South Florida, 1822–1840, Part I: Key West Phase." *Tequesta* 40 (1980): 47–77.

———. "Richard Fitzpatrick's South Florida, 1822–1840, Part II: Fitzpatrick's Miami River Plantation." *Tequesta* 41 (1981): 33–68.

Blackman, Ethan. *Miami and Dade County, Florida: Its Settlement, Progress and Achievement.* Washington, DC: V. Rainbolt, 1921.

Blank, Joan Gill. *Key Biscayne.* Sarasota: Pineapple Press, 1996.

Bonath, Shawn. "Archaeological Research Strategy for the Granada Site." *FA* 33 (1980): 32–44.

Bonawit, Oby J. *Miami, Florida Early Families, and Records.* Miami: Bonawit, 1980.

Braund, Kathryn E. Holland. "The Creek Indians, Blacks, and Slavery." *Journal of Southern History* 57 (1991): 601–636.

Brickell, Beth. *William and Mary Brickell: Founders of Miami and Fort Lauderdale.* Charleston, SC: History Press, 2011.

Brooks, Abbie. *The Unwritten History of St. Augustine.* St. Augustine: Record Company, 1909.

Brown, Canter, Jr. *Florida's Peace River Frontier.* Orlando: University of Central Florida Press, 1991.

———. "Race Relations in Territorial Florida, 1821–1845." *FHQ* 73 (1995): 287–307.

Buck, James. "Biscayne Sketches at the Far South." *Tequesta* 9 (1949): 70–86.

Buker, George E. "The Mosquito Fleet's Guides and the Second Seminole War." *FHQ* 57 (1979): 308–326.

Bullen, Adelaide K. *Florida Indians of Past and Present.* Gainesville: Kendall Books, 1965.

Burkhardt, Mrs. Henry J. "Starch Making: A Florida Pioneer Industry." *Tequesta* 12 (1952): 47–53.

Bushnell, Amy Turner. "Ruling 'the Republic of Indians' in Seventeenth-Century Florida." In *Powhatan's Mantle: Indians in the Colonial South,* edited by Peter Wood, Gregory Waselkov, and Thomas Hatley, 134–150. Lincoln: University of Nebraska Press, 1989.

Calloway, Colin. *One Vast Winter Count: The Native American West before Lewis and Clark.* Lincoln: University of Nebraska Press, 2003.

Campbell, John. "The Seminoles, the 'Bloodhounds' and Abolitionism, 1796–1865." *Journal of Southern History* 72 (2006): 259–302.

Canova, Andrew P. *Life and Adventures in South Florida.* Tampa: Tribune Printing Company, 1906.

Carballido y Zúñiga, Andrés González de Barcía. *Chronological History of the Continent of Florida.* . . . Gainesville: University Press of Florida, 1951.

Carr, Robert S. "The Brickell Store and Seminole Trade." *FA* 34 (1981): 180–199.

———. *Digging Miami.* Gainesville: University Press of Florida, 2012.

———. "Early Man in South Florida." *Archaeology* 40 (1987): 62–63.

Carr, Robert S., and John F. Reiger. "Strombus Celt Caches in Southeast Florida." *FA* 33 (1980): 66–74.

Carr, Robert S., Willard S. Steele, and Peter Stone. *A Phase II Archaeological Survey and Assessment of the Weston Pond Site, 8BD2132, Broward County, Florida.* Technical Report No. 72. Miami: Archaeological and Historical Conservancy, 1993.

Carr, Robert S., Jorge Zamanillo, and Willard S. Steele. *An Archaeological Survey of Southeast Broward County, Florida: Phase 3.* Technical Report No. 117. Miami: Archaeological and Historical Conservancy, 1995.

Carson, Ruby Lee. "Miami: 1896 to 1900." *Tequesta* 16 (1956): 5–6.

Carter, Clarence Edwin, ed. *The Territorial Papers of the United States.* Washington, DC: Government Printing Office, 1934–.

Cash, W. T. "The Lower East Coast, 1870–1890." *Tequesta* 8 (1948): 57–71.

*Causes of Hostilities of Seminole Indians.* U.S. House of Representatives. H. Executive Doc. 267. 24th Congress, 1st Session, 1836.

Chardon, Roland E. "The Cape Florida Society of 1773." *Tequesta* 35 (1975): 75–88.

———. "Northern Biscayne Bay in 1776." *Tequesta* 35 (1975): 37–74.

Childers, R. Wayne. "Life in Miami and the Keys: Two Reports and a Map from the Monaco Alaña Mission, 1743." *FHQ* 82 (2003): 59–82.

*Claim of Richard Fitzpatrick.* U.S. Senate. *S. Report No. 234,* 32nd Congress, 1st Session, 1852.

Clark, Patricia. "Florida 'Our Own Italy': James F. B. Marshall's Post-Civil War Letters to Edward Everett Hale." *FHQ* 59 (1980): 53–71.

Coffman, Edward M. *The Old Army: A Portrait of the American Army in Peacetime, 1784–1898.* New York: Oxford University Press, 1988.

Coker, William S., and Thomas D. Watson. *Indian Traders of the Southeastern Spanish Borderlands: Panton, Leslie and Company and John Forbes and Company, 1783–1847.* Pensacola: University of West Florida Press, 1986.

Connolly, Nathan. *A World More Concrete: Real Estate and the Remaking of Jim Crow South Florida.* Chicago: University of Chicago Press, 2014.

Connor, Jeannette Thurber. *Colonial Records of Spanish Florida: Letters and Reports of Governors and Secular Persons.* 2 vols. Tallahassee: Florida State Historical Society, 1925.

Covington, James W. *The Billy Bowlegs War, 1855–1858: The Final Stand of the Seminoles against the Whites.* Chuluota, FL: Mickler House: 1982.

———. *The Seminoles of Florida.* Gainesville: University Press of Florida, 1993.

———. "Trade Relations between Southwestern Florida and Cuba: 1600–1840." *FHQ* 38 (1959): 114–128.

Crane, Verner W. *The Southern Frontier, 1670–1732*. Ann Arbor: University of Michigan Press, 1929.

Craton, Michael, and Gail Saunders. *A History of the Bahamian People: From Aboriginal Times to the End of Slavery*. Athens: University of Georgia Press, 1999.

Cronon, William. *Changes in the Land: Indians, Colonists, and the Ecology of New England*. New York: Hill and Wang, 2003.

———. *Nature's Metropolis: Chicago and the Great West*. New York: Norton, 1991.

Crosby, Alfred W., Jr. *Columbian Exchange: Biological and Cultural Consequences of 1492*. Westport, CT: Greenwood, 1972.

Cumming, William Patterson. *The Southeast in Early Maps: With an Annotated Check List of Printed and Manuscript Regional and Local Maps of Southeastern North America during the Colonial Period*. Chapel Hill: University of North Carolina Press, 1962.

Cusick, James. *The Other War of 1812: The Patriot War and the American Invasion of Spanish East Florida*. Gainesville: University Press of Florida, 2003.

Davenport, Will. "Growing Up, Sort of, in Miami." *Tequesta* 39 (1979): 5–29.

Davies, K. G., ed. *Calendar of State Papers, Colonial Series, America and West Indies, Preserved in the Public Records Office*. London: Her Majesty's Stationery Office, 1969.

Davis, T. Frederick. "Juan Ponce de Leon's First Voyage and Discovery of Florida." *FHQ* 14 (1935): 7–49.

De Brahm, John William Gerard. *Atlantic Pilot*. London: Printed for the Author, 1772.

———. *Report of the General Survey in the Southern District of North America*. Edited by Louis De Vorsey Jr. Columbia: University of South Carolina Press, 1971.

Denham, James M. *"A Rogue's Paradise": Crime and Punishment in Antebellum Florida, 1821–1861*. Tuscaloosa: University of Alabama Press, 1997.

Dillon, Rodney E., Jr. "Gang of Pirates: Confederate Lighthouse Raids in Southeast Florida, 1861." *FHQ* 67 (1989): 441–457.

———. "South Florida in 1860." 60 *FHQ* (1982): 440–454.

Dixon, Jacqueline Eaby, Kyla Simons, Loretta Leist, Christopher Eck, John

Ricisak, John Gifford, and Jeff Ryan. "Provenance of Stone Celts from the Miami Circle Archaeological Site, Miami, Florida." *FA* (2000): 328–341.

Dodd, Dorothy, ed. *Florida Becomes a State*. Tallahassee: Florida Centennial Commission, 1945.

———. "The Wrecking Business on the Florida Reef, 1822–1860." *FHQ* 22 (1944): 171–199.

Doran, Glen, *Windover: Multidisciplinary Investigations of an Early Archaic Florida Cemetery*. Gainesville: University Press of Florida, 2002.

Dorn, J. K. "Recollections of Early Miami." *Tequesta* 9 (1949): 43–60.

Douglas, Marjory Stoneman. *The Everglades: River of Grass*. New York: Rinehart and Company, 1947.

Dunbar, James S. *Paleoindian Societies of the Coastal Southeast*. Gainesville: University Press of Florida, 2016.

Eck, Christopher R., ed. "South Florida's Prelude to War." *Tequesta* 62 (2002): 68–115.

Ellicott, Andrew. *The Journal of Andrew Ellicott: Late Commissioner on Behalf of the United States*. Philadelphia: Bud and Bartram, 1803.

Ethridge, Robbie. *From Chicaza to Chickasaw: The European Invasion and the Transformation of the Mississippian World, 1540–1715*. Chapel Hill: University of North Carolina Press, 2010.

Ethridge, Robbie, and Sheri M. Shuck-Hall, eds. *Mapping the Mississippian Shatter Zone: The Colonial Indian Slave Trade and Regional Instability in the American South*. Lincoln: University of Nebraska Press, 2009.

*The First Thirty Years of Miami and the Bank of Bay Biscayne*. Miami: Bank of Bay Biscayne, 1926.

*Florida Facts for Tourists: Authentic Information concerning the State*. Tallahassee: Department of Agriculture, ca. 1930.

*Florida: Pennsylvania Railroad Company*. Philadelphia: Allen, Lane, and Scott, 1896.

Fontaneda, Hernando d'Escalante. *Fontaneda's Memoir*. Edited by David O. True and translated by Buckingham Smith. Miami: University of Miami and Historical Association of South Florida Reprints, 1945.

Forbes, James Grant. *Sketches, Historical and Topographical of the Florida, More Particularly East Florida*. New York: C. S. Van Winkle, 1821.

*Fort Dallas (William English Plantation) Designation Report*. Miami: City of Miami, 1984.

Frank, Andrew K. "Creating a Seminole Enemy: Ethnic and Racial Diversity in the Conquest of Florida." *Florida International University Law Review* 9 (2014): 277–293.

———. *Creeks and Southerners: Biculturalism on the Early American Frontier.* Lincoln: University of Nebraska Press, 2005.

———. "Preserving the Path of Peace: White Plumes and Diplomacy during the Frontier Panic of 1849–1850." *Journal of Florida Studies* 1 (Spring 2013), http://www.journaloffloridastudies.org/0102pathofpeace.html.

———. "Taking the State Out: Seminoles and Creeks at a Transnational Moment." *FHQ* 84 (2005): 10–27.

Frazier, James C. "Samuel Touchett's Florida Plantation." *Tequesta* 35 (1975): 75–88.

Fuente, Alejandro de la. *Havana and the Atlantic in the Sixteenth Century.* Chapel Hill: University of North Carolina Press, 2008.

Fuson, Robert H. *Juan Ponce de León and the Discovery of Puerto Rico and Florida.* New York: McDonald and Woodward Publishing Co, 2000.

Gallay, Alan. *The Indian Slave Trade: The Rise of the English Empire in the American South.* New Haven: Yale University Press, 2003.

Gannon, Michael. *Florida: A Short History.* Gainesville: University Press of Florida, 2003.

Gatschet, Albert Samuel. *A Creek Migration Legend: With a Linguistic, Historic and Ethnographic Introduction.* Philadelphia: D. G. Brinton, 1884.

George, Paul S. *Along the Miami River.* Charleston, SC: Arcadia Books, 2013.

———. "Passage to the New Eden: Tourism in Miami from Flagler to Everest G. Sewell." 59 *FHQ* (1981): 440–463.

Goggin, John Mann. "Cultural Traditions in Florida Prehistory." In *The Florida Indian and His Neighbors*, edited by John W. Griffin, 13–44. Winter Park, FL: Rollins College, 1949.

———. "The Tekesta Indians of Southern Florida." *FHQ* 18 (1940): 274–284.

Goggin, John Mann, and William C. Sturtevant. "The Calusa, a Stratified, Non-Agricultural Society (with Notes on Sibling Marriage)." In *Explorations in Cultural Anthropology: Essays in Honor of George Peter Murdock*, edited by Ward H. Goodenough, 179–219. New York: McGraw-Hill, 1964.

*Golden Days on the East Coast of Florida.* St. Augustine: Florida East Coast Railroad, 1927.

Granberry, Julien. "The Position of the Calusa Language in Florida Prehistory: A Hypothesis." *FA* 48 (1995): 156–173.

Griffin, John. *Archaeology of the Everglades.* Edited by Jerald T. Milanich and James J. Miller. Gainesville: University Press of Florida, 2002.

Griffin, John W., Sue B. Richardson, Mary Pohl, Carl D. McMurray, C. Margaret Scarry, Suzanne K. Fish, Elizabeth S. Wing, L. Jill Loucks, and Marcia K. Welsh, eds. *Excavations at the Granada Site: Archaeology and History of the Granada Site.* 2 vols. Tallahassee: Florida Division of Archives, History and Records Management, 1985.

Hamilton, Frank. "Spanish Land Grants in Florida." *FHQ* 20 (1941): 77–81.

Hammond, Benjamin. "The Tropical Laboratory at Miami and Some Other Things." *American Gardener* (May 3, 1902): 288.

Hammond, E. A. "Dr. Strobel Reports on Southeast Florida." *Tequesta* 21 (1961): 65–75.

————, ed. "Sketches of the Florida Keys, 1829–1833." *Tequesta* 30 (1970): 73–94.

————. "Wreckers and Wrecking on the Florida Reef, 1829–1832." *FHQ* 41 (1963): 239–273.

Hann, John H. *Indians of Central and South Florida: 1513–1763.* Gainesville: University Press of Florida, 2003.

————. *Missions to the Calusa.* Gainesville: University Press of Florida, 1991.

————. "Summary Guide to Spanish Florida Missions and Visitas: With Churches in the Sixteenth and Seventeenth Centuries." *Americas* 46 (1990): 417–513.

Hanna, A. J. "The Escape of the Confederate Secretary of War John Cabell Breckinridge as Revealed by His Diary." *Register of the Kentucky State Historical Society* 37 (1939): 323–333.

Harper, Roland M. "Agricultural Conditions in Florida in 1925." *Economic Geography* 3 (1927): 340–353.

Hemmings, C. Andrew. "The Paleoindian and Early Archaic Tools of Sloth Hole (8Je121): An Inundated Site in the Lower Aucilla River, Jefferson County, Florida." MA thesis, University of Florida, 1999.

Herrera y Tordesilla, Antonio. *Historia general de los hechos de los castellanos en las islas i tierra firme de Mar Oceano.* Madrid: En la imprenta real de Nicola Rodiquez Franco, 1726.

*Historical Fort Dallas.* Miami: Miami Metropolis, 1897.

Hoffer, Peter C. *Law and People in Colonial America.* Baltimore: Johns Hopkins University Press, 1998.

Hoffman, Paul E. *Florida's Frontiers (A History of the Trans-Appalachian).* Bloomington: University of Indiana Press, 2002.

———. *The Spanish Crown and the Defense of the Caribbean, 1535–1585: Precedent, Patrimonialism, and Royal Parsimony.* Baton Rouge: Louisiana State University Press, 1980.

———. "Until the Land Was Understood: Spaniards Confront La Florida, 1500–1600." In *La Florida: Five Hundred Years of Hispanic Presence,* edited by Viviana Díaz Balsera and Rachel A. May, 69–82. Gainesville: University Press of Florida, 2013.

Hoffmeister, J. E. *Land from the Sea: The Geologic Story of South Florida.* Coral Gables: University of Miami Press, 1974.

Hoole, W. Stanley. ed. *Florida Territory in 1844: The Diary of Master Edward C. Anderson.* University: University of Alabama Press, 1977.

Howard, Rosalyn A. *Black Seminoles in the Bahamas.* Gainesville: University Press of Florida, 2002.

———. "The 'Wild Indians' of Andros Island: Black Seminole Legacy in the Bahamas." *Journal of Black Studies* 37 (2006): 275–298.

Hudson, F. M. "The Beginnings of Dade County." *Tequesta* 3 (1943): 1–35.

Ives, J. C. *Memoir to Accompany a Military Map of Florida, South of Tampa Bay.* New York: M. B. Wynkoop, 1856.

Jackson, Jason Baird. "Seminole Histories of the Calusa." *Native South* 7 (2014): 122–142.

Jasanoff, Maya. *Liberty's Exiles: American Loyalists in the Revolutionary World.* New York: Knopf, 2011.

Johnson, Howard. *The Bahamas from Slavery to Servitude, 1783–1933.* Gainesville: University Press of Florida, 1996.

Johnson, Walter. *River of Dark Dreams: Slavery and Empire in the Cotton Kingdom.* Cambridge, MA: Harvard University Press 2013.

*Journal of the Commissioners for Trade and Plantations.* 14 vols. London: H. M. Stationery Office, 1920–1928.

*A Journal of the Proceedings of the Legislative Council of the Territory of Florida, at Its Thirteenth Session.* Tallahassee: Printed at the Office of the *Floridian,* 1835.

Judd, Richard W. *Second Nature: An Environmental History of New England.* Amherst: University of Massachusetts Press, 2014.

Kappler, Charles. *Indian Affairs: Laws and Treaties.* 7 vols. Washington, DC: Government Printing Office, 1904.

Keegan, William F. *The People Who Discovered Columbus: The Prehistory of the Bahamas.* Gainesville: University Press of Florida, 1992.

Kelly, James E., Jr. "Juan Ponce de Leon's Discovery of Florida: Herrera's Narrative Revisited." *Revista de Historia de America* 111 (1991): 30–65.

Kelton, Paul. *Epidemics and Enslavement: Biological Catastrophe in the Native Southeast, 1492–1715.* Lincoln: University of Nebraska Press, 2007.

Kenny, Michael. *Romance of the Floridas: The Finding and the Founding.* New York: Bruce Publishing Company, 1934.

Kersey, Harry A., Jr. "The Havana Connection: Buffalo Tiger, Fidel Castro, and the Origin of Miccosukee Tribal Sovereignty, 1959–1962." *American Indian Quarterly* 25 (2001): 491–507.

———. *Pelts, Plumes, and Hides: White Traders among the Seminole Indians, 1870–1930.* Gainesville: University Press of Florida, 1975.

———. "The Seminole Negroes of Andros Island Revisited: Some New Pieces to an Old Puzzle." *FA* 34 (1981): 169–176.

Kersey, Harry A., Jr., and Helen M. Bannan. "Patchwork and Politics: The Evolving Roles of Florida Seminole Women in the Twentieth Century." In *Negotiators of Change: Historical Perspectives on Native American Women,* edited by Nancy Shoemaker, 193–212. New York: Routledge, 1995.

Kinnaird, Lawrence. "The Significance of William Augustus Bowles' Seizure of Panton's Apalachee Store in 1792." *FHQ* 9 (1931): 156–192.

Kirk, Cooper. "William Cooley: A Broward Legend." *Broward Legacy* 1 (1976): 12–20.

Kolianos, Phyllis E., and Brent R. Weisman, eds. *Florida Journals of Frank Hamilton Cushing.* Gainesville: University Press of Florida, 2005.

Krech, Shephard, III. *The Ecological Indian: Myth and History.* New York: Norton, 1999.

Kropp, Phoebe. *Adobe Vieja: Culture and Memory in a Modern American Place.* Berkeley: University of California Press, 2008.

*Land Claims in East Florida, Communicated to the House of Representatives, February 23, 1826.* Washington, DC: Government Printing Office, 1826.

Larson, Lewis H. *Aboriginal Subsistence Technology on the Southeastern Coastal Plain during the Late Prehistoric Period.* Gainesville: University Press of Florida, 1980.

Laudonnière, René Goulaine de. *Three Voyages.* Translated by Charles E. Bennett. Tuscaloosa: University of Alabama Press, 2001.

Laxon, D. D. "The Dupont Plaza Site." *Florida Anthropologist* 21 (June 1968): 55–60.

Ledin, R. Bruce. "Tropical and Subtropical Fruits in Florida (Other Than Citrus)." *Economic Botany* 11 (1957): 350.

*Letters of Jefferson Davis, October 1863–August 1864*. Edited by Lynda L. Crist, Kenneth H. Williams, and Peggy L. Dillard. Vol. 10. Baton Rouge: Louisiana State University Press, 1999.

Levin, Ted. *Liquid Land: A History: A Journey through the Florida Everglades*. Athens: University of Georgia Press, 2003.

Lewis, Clifford M. "The Calusa." In *Tacachale: Essays on the Indians of Florida and Southeastern Georgia during the Historic Period*, edited by Jerald R. Milanich and Samuel Proctor, 19–49. Gainesville: University Press of Florida, 1978.

Lewis, David Rich. *Neither Wolf Nor Dog: American Indians, Environment, and Agrarian Change*. New York: Oxford University Press, 1994.

*List of Vessels Captured and Destroyed for Violation of Blockade or in Battle, May 1861 to May 1865*. U.S. House of Representatives. H.R. Document 91/2, 54th Congress, 1st Session, 1896.

Lowery, Woodbury. *The Spanish Settlements within the Present Limits of the United States: Florida, 1562–1574*. New York: G. P. Putnam and Sons, 1905.

Luer, George M. "Calusa Canals in Southwestern Florida: Routes of Tribute and Exchange." *FA* 42 (1989): 89–130.

Luer, George M., and Ryan J. Wheeler. "How the Pine Island Canal Worked: Topography, Hydraulics, and Engineering." *FA* 50 (1997): 115–131.

Lyon, Eugene. *The Enterprise of Florida: Pedro Menéndez de Avilés and the Spanish Conquest of 1565–1568*. Gainesville: University Press of Florida, 1976.

———. "The Florida Mutineers, 1566–1567." *Tequesta* 44 (1984): 44–61.

———. "Pedro Menéndez's Strategic Plan for the Florida Peninsula." 67 *FHQ* (1988): 1–14.

MacCauley, Clay. *The Seminole Indians of Florida*. Gainesville: University Press of Florida, 2000.

Mahon, John. *History of the Second Seminole War, 1835–1842*. Gainesville: University Press of Florida, 1967.

Marchman, Walt P. "The Ingraham Everglades Exploring Expedition, 1892." *Tequesta* 7 (1947): 3–43.

Marks, Henry S. "A Forgotten Spanish Land Grant in South Florida." *Tequesta* 20 (1960): 51–55.

Marotti, Frank, Jr. *The Cana Sanctuary: History, Diplomacy, and Black Catholic Marriage in Antebellum St. Augustine*. Tuscaloosa: University of Alabama Press, 2012.

———. *Heaven's Soldiers: Free People of Color and the Spanish Legacy in Antebellum Florida*. Tuscaloosa: University of Alabama Press, 2013.

Martin, Sidney Walter. *Florida's Flagler*. Athens: University of Georgia Press, 1949.

McCally, David. *The Everglades: An Environmental History*. Gainesville: University Press of Florida, 1999.

McDonough, Mark A. *The Francis Richard Family: From French Nobility to Florida Pioneers*. Lulu.com, 2011.

McGoun, William E. *Ancient Miamians*. Gainesville: University Press of Florida, 2002.

———. *Prehistoric Peoples of South Florida*. Tuscaloosa: University of Alabama Press, 1993.

McIver, Stuart B. *Touched by the Sun*. Sarasota: Pineapple Press, 2001.

McLendon, James. *Pioneer in the Florida Keys: The Life and Times of Del Layton*. Key West: E. A. Seemann Publishers, 1976.

McNeill, Wilfred T. "Sailing Vessels of the Florida Seminole." *FA* 9 (1956): 79–86.

McNicoll, Robert E. "Caloosa Village *Tequesta*: A Miami of the Sixteenth Century." *Tequesta* 1 (1941): 11–20.

Melish, John. *A Description of East and West Florida and the Bahama Islands, with an Account of the Most Important Places in the United States, Bordering upon Florida and the Gulf of Mexico. . . .* Philadelphia: G. Palmer, 1813.

Meltzer, David J. *First Peoples in a New World: Colonizing Ice Age America*. Berkeley: University of California Press, 2009.

Merás, Gonzalo Solís de. *Pedro Menéndez de Avilés, Memorial*. Translated by Jeannette Thurber Conner. Gainesville: University Press of Florida, 1923.

Metropolitan Dade County Office of Community Development. *From Wilderness to Metropolis: The History and Architecture of Dade County (1825–1940)*. Miami: Metropolitan Dade County, 1982.

Milanich, Jerald T. *Archaeology of Precolumbian Florida*. Gainesville: University Press of Florida, 1994.

———. "Charting Juan Ponce de León's 1513 Voyage to Florida: The Calusa Indians amid Latitudes of Controversy." In *La Florida: 500 Years of Hispanic Presence*, edited by Viviana Díaz Balsera and Rachel A. May, 49–68. Gainesville: University Press of Florida, 2013.

———. *Florida Indians: Ancient Times to Present*. Gainesville: University Press of Florida, 1998.

———. *Florida Indians and the Invasion from Europe*. Gainesville: University Press of Florida, 1995.

———. *Hernando de Soto and the Indians of Florida*. Gainesville: University Press of Florida, 1998.

———. *Laboring in the Fields of the Lord: Spanish Missions in Southeastern Indians*. Washington, DC: Smithsonian Institution Press, 1999.

———. *The Timucua*. Oxford, UK: Wiley-Blackwell, 1996.

Milanich, Jerald T., and Nara B. Milanich. "Revisiting the Freducci Map: A Description of Juan Ponce de Leon's 1513 Florida Voyage?" *FHQ* 74 (1996): 319–328.

*Military Map of the Peninsula of Florida, South of Tampa Bay*. New York: M. B. Wynkoop, 1856.

Miller, Robert J. "The Doctrine of Discovery, Manifest Destiny, and American Indians." In *Why You Can't Teach United States History without American Indians*, edited by Susan Sleeper-Smith, Juliana Barr, Jean M. O'Brien, Nancy Shoemaker, and Scott Manning Stevens, 87–100. Chapel Hill: University of North Carolina Press, 2015.

Miller, Robert J., Jacinta Ruru, Larissa Behrendt, and Tracey Lindberg. *Discovering Indigenous Lands: The Doctrine of Discovery in the English Colonies*. New York: Oxford University Press, 2010.

Mohl, Raymond. "Black Immigrants: Bahamians in Early Twentieth-Century Miami." *FHQ* 65 (1987): 271–297.

Mormino, Gary R. *Land of Sunshine, State of Dreams: A Social History of Modern Florida*. Gainesville: University Press of Florida, 2008.

———. "So Many Residents, So Few Floridians." *Forum: The Magazine of the Florida Humanities Council* 33 (Spring 2009): 38–40.

Motte, Jacob Rhett. *Journey into Wilderness: An Army Surgeon's Account of Life in Camp and Field during the Creek and Seminole Wars 1836–1838*. Edited by James F. Sunderman. Gainesville: University of Florida Press, 1953.

Mowat, Charles L. "That Odd Being De Brahm." *FHQ* 29 (1942): 323–345.

Muir, Helen. *Miami U.S.A.* Gainesville: University Press of Florida, 2000.

Munroe, Kirk. *Through Swamp and Glade: A Tale of the Seminole War.* New York: Scribner's, 1896.

Murdoch, Richard K. "Documents concerning a Voyage to the Miami Region in 1793." *FHQ* 31 (1952): 16–32.

Myers, Ronald L., and John J. Ewel. *Ecosystems of Florida.* Orlando: University of Central Florida Press, 1990.

Narrett, David E. *Adventurism and Empire: The Struggle for Mastery in the Louisiana-Florida Borderlands, 1792–1803.* Chapel Hill: University of North Carolina Press, 2015.

Nellis, David W. *Poisonous Plants and Animals of Florida and the Caribbean.* Sarasota: Pineapple Press, 1997.

Nordhoff, Charles. "Wrecking on the Florida Keys." *Harper's Magazine* 18 (April 1859): 583–585.

Norton, Charles Ledyard. *A Handbook of Florida.* New York: Longmans and Green, 1891.

O'Brien, Jean M. *Firsting and Lasting: Writing Indians out of Existence in New England.* Minneapolis: University of Minnesota Press, 2010.

Ortiz, Stephen. *Reconstruction Betrayed: The Hidden History of Black Organizing and White Violence in Florida from Reconstruction to the Bloody Election of 1920.* Berkeley: University of California Press 2005.

Parker, Susan R. "Men without God or King: Rural Settlers of East Florida, 1784–1790." *FHQ* 69 (1990): 135–155.

Parks, Arva Moore. "The History of Coconut Grove, Florida: 1821–1925." M.A. thesis, University of Miami, 1971.

———. "Miami in 1876." *Tequesta* 35 (1975): 89–145.

———. *Miami: The Magic City.* Tulsa: Continental Heritage Press, 1981.

———. *Where the River Found the Bay: Historical Study of the Granada Site, Miami, Florida.* Vol. 2 of *Excavations at the Granada Site: Archaeology and History of the Granada Site,* edited by John W. Griffin et al. Tallahassee: Florida Division of Archives, History and Records Management, 1985.

Peck, Douglas T. "Reconstruction and Analysis of the 1513 Discovery Voyage of Juan Ponce de Leon." *FHQ* 71 (1992): 133–154.

Perrine, Henry. *Biscayne Bay, Dade Co. Florida: Between the 25th and 26th Degrees of Latitude.* Albany: Weed, Parsons and Company, 1876.

Peters, Thelma. *Miami, 1909: With Excerpts from Fannie Clemons' Diary.* Miami: Banyan Books, 1984.

*Pictorial History of the Florida Hurricane, September 18, 1929.* Miami: Tyler Publishing, 1926.

Pittman, Craig, and Matthew Waite. *Paving Paradise: Florida's Vanishing Wetlands and the Failure of No Net Loss.* Gainesville: University Press of Florida, 2010.

Poitrineau, Abel. "Demography and the Political Destiny of Florida during the Second Spanish Period." *FHQ* 66 (1988): 420–433.

Poole, Leslie Kemp. *Saving Florida: Women's Fight for the Environment in the Twentieth Century.* Gainesville: University Press of Florida, 2015.

Porter, Kenneth W. "Negroes and the Seminole War, 1817–1818." *Journal of Negro History* 36 (1951): 249–280.

———. "Notes on Seminole Negroes in the Bahamas." *FHQ* 24 (1945): 56–60.

Portes, Alejandro, and Alex Stepick. *City on the Edge: The Transformation of Miami.* Berkeley: University of California Press, 1993.

Pozzetta, George. "Foreign Colonies in South Florida, 1865–1910." *Tequesta* 24 (1974): 45–56.

*Proceedings of the Military Court of Inquiry in the Case of Maj. Gen. Scott.* Washington, DC: Gales and Seaton, 1837.

Purdy, Barbara A. *The Art and Archaeology of Florida's Wetlands.* Boca Raton: CRC Press, 1991.

———. *Florida's People during the Last Ice Age.* Gainesville: University Press of Florida, 2008.

Purdy, Barbara A., Kevin S. Jones, John J. Mecholsky, Gerald Bourne, Richard C. Hulbert Jr., Bruce J. MacFadden, Krista L. Church, Michael W. Warren, Thomas F. Jorstad, Dennis J. Stanford, Melvin J. Wachowiak, Robert J. Speakman, et al. "Earliest Art in the Americas: Incised Image of a Proboscidean on a Mineralized Extinct Animal Bone from Vero Beach, Florida." *Journal of Archaeological Science* 38 (2011): 2908–2913.

Rainbolt, Victor. *The Town That Climate Built: The Story of the Rise of a City in the American Tropics.* Miami: Parker Art Printing Association, 1924.

Randazzo, A. F., and D. S. Jones, eds. *The Geology of Florida.* Gainesville: University Press of Florida, 1997.

Reavis, L. U. *The Life and Military Service of Gen. William Selby Harney.* St. Louis: Bryan, Brand and Company, 1878.

Reed, John Shelton. "South But Not Southern." *Forum: The Magazine of the Florida Humanities Council* 27 (Fall 2003): 10.

Reilly, Benjamin. *Tropical Surge: A History of Ambition and Disaster on the Florida Shore.* Sarasota: Pineapple Press, 2005.

*Reports of the Courts of Claims.* U.S. House of Representatives. *H.R. Report No. 175,* 35th Congress, 1st session, May 14, 1858.

Revels, Tracy J. *Sunshine Paradise: A History of Florida Tourism.* Gainesville: University Press of Florida, 2011.

Ribas, Andrés Pérez de. *My Life among the Savage Indians of New Spain.* Translated by Tomás Antonio Robertson. Los Angeles, CA: Ward Ritchie Press, 1968.

Richter, Daniel K. *Before the Revolution: America's Ancient Pasts.* Cambridge, MA: Harvard University Press, 2011.

Riordan, Patrick. "Finding Freedom in Florida: Native Peoples, African Americans and Colonists, 1670–1815." *FHQ* 75 (1995): 24–43.

Rivers, Larry Eugene. *Rebels and Runaways: Slave Resistance in Nineteenth-Century Florida.* Urbana: University of Illinois Press, 2013.

——— *Slavery in Florida: Territorial Days to Emancipation.* Gainesville: University Press of Florida, 2008.

Roberts, Cecil. *Gone Sunwards.* New York: Macmillan Company: 1936.

Roberts, Charles, and George Gauld. *A Chart of the Gulf of Florida or New Bahama Channel....* London: Printed for William Faden, 1794.

Roberts, William. *An Account of the First Discovery and Natural History of Florida.* Facsimile reproduction of 1763 ed. Gainesville: University Press of Florida, 1976.

Robinson, A. A. *The Resources and Natural Advantages of Florida: Containing Special Papers Descriptive of the Several Counties.* Tallahassee: Floridian Book and Job Office, 1882.

Romans, Bernard. *A Concise Natural History of East and West Florida.* New York: For the Author, 1775.

Ross, Daniel J. J., and Bruce S. Chappell. "Visit to the Indian Nations." *FHQ* 55 (1976): 60–73.

Ruidíaz y Caravia, *La Florida: Su conquista y colonización por Pedro Menéndez de Avilés.* 2 vols. Madrid: Imp. de los Hijos de J. A. García, 1893.

Sauer, Carl Ortwin. *Sixteenth Century North America: The Land and People as Seen by the Europeans.* Berkeley: University of California Press, 1971.

Saunders, Gail. *Bahamian Loyalists and Their Slaves.* London: Macmillan Caribbean, 1983.

Scarry, C. Margaret. "Paleoethnobotany of the Granada Site." In *Excavations at the Granada Site: Archaeology and History of the Granada Site,* edited by John W. Griffin et al., 1:232–233. 2 vols. Tallahassee: Florida Division of Archives, History and Records Management, 1985.

Scarry, C. Margaret, and Lee A. Newsom. "Archaeobotanical Research in the Calusa Heartland." In *Culture and Environment in the Domain of the Calusa*, edited by William H. Marquardt, 375–402. Gainesville: Institute of Archaeology and Paleoenvironmental Studies, 1992.

Schafer, Daniel L. "Early Plantation Development in British East Florida." *El Escribano* 19 (1982): 37–53.

———. *William Bartram and the Ghost Plantations of British East Florida.* Gainesville: University Press of Florida, 2010.

*Seminole Hostilities.* U.S. House of Representatives. H.R. Doc. No. 271, 24th Congress, 1st Session, 1836.

Sewell, John. *Memoirs and History of Miami, Florida.* Miami: Franklin Press, 1933.

Shapee, Nathan D. "Fort Dallas and the Naval Depot on Key Biscayne, 1836–1926." *Tequesta* 21 (1961): 13–40.

Shea, John Gilmary. "Ancient Florida." In *Narrative and Critical History of America*, ed. Justin Winsor, 2:231–298. 5 vols. Boston: Houghton Mifflin and Company, 1884–1889.

Siebert, Wilbur Henry. *The Legacy of the American Revolution to the British West Indies and Bahamas.* Columbus: Ohio State University, 1913.

———. *Loyalists in East Florida, 1774–1785.* 2 vols. Deland: Florida State Historical Society, 1929.

Simpson, Charles Torrye. *Ornamental Gardening in Florida.* Little River, FL: The Author, 1916.

Small, John K. "Seminole Bread–The Conti." *Journal of the New York Botanical Garden* 22 (July 1921): 121–137.

Smith, Hale G. "Ethnological and Archaeological Significance of Zamia." *American Anthropologist* 53 (1951): 240–242.

*Spanish Land Grants in Florida: Briefed Translations from the Archives of the Board of Commissioners for Ascertaining Claims and Titles to Land in the Territory of Florida.* 5 vols. Tallahassee: State Library Board, 1940–1941.

Standiford, Les. *Last Train to Paradise: Henry Flagler and the Spectacular Rise and Fall of the Railroad that Crossed an Ocean.* New York: Broadway Books, 2003.

Stebbins, Consuelo. *City of Intrigue, Nest of Revolution: A Documentary History of Key West in the Nineteenth Century.* Gainesville: University Press of Florida, 2007.

Stephens, I. J. "The Port of Miami." *Update* 2 (June 1975): 3, 12.

Stepick, Alex, Guillermo Grenier, Max Castro, and Marvin Dunn. *This Land*

*Is Our Land: Immigrants and Power in Miami.* Berkeley: University of California Press, 2003.

Sternhell, Yael A. *Routes to War: The World of Movement in the Confederate South.* Cambridge, MA: Harvard University Press, 2012.

Straight, William M. "Early Miami through the Eyes of Youth." *Tequesta* 63 (2003): 62–76.

Sturtevant, William C. "Chakaika and the Spanish Indians: Documentary Evidence Compared with Seminole Sources." *Tequesta* 13 (1955): 35–73.

———. "The Last of the South Florida Aborigines." In *Tacachale: Essays on the Indians of Florida and Southeastern Georgia during the Historic Period,* ed. Jerald R. Milanich and Samuel Proctor, 141–162. Gainesville: University Press of Florida, 1978.

———. "A Seminole Personal Document." *Tequesta* 16 (1956): 55–75.

Swanson, Gail. *Documentation of the Indians of the Florida Keys and Miami, 1513–1765.* Haverford, PA: Infinity Publishing, 2003.

Swanton, John R. *Early History of the Creek Indians and Their Neighbors.* Gainesville: University Press of Florida, 1989.

Townshend, F. Trench. *Wild Life in Florida, with a Visit to Cuba.* London: Hurst and Blackett, Publishers, 1875.

True, David O. "The Freducci Map of 1514–1515: What It Discloses of Early Florida History." *Tequesta* 4 (1944): 50–55.

———. "Some Early Maps Relating to Florida." *Imago Mundi* 11 (1954): 73–84.

Tuttle, Julia [Mrs E. R. Sturtevant]. "Life in Dade County." *Semi-Tropical* 2 (April 1876): 203–204.

Ugarte, Rúben Vargas. "First Jesuit Missions in Florida." *Historical Records and Studies: U.S. Catholic Historical Society* 25 (1935): 59–148.

———. *Los mártires de la Florida, 1566–1572.* Lima: [Talleres Gráficos de la Editorial "Lumen," SA,] 1940.

van Deman, H. W. "Fruits in Southern Florida." *Colman's Rural World* (April 16, 1914): 4.

Vega, Garcilasco de la. *Florida of the Inca.* Translated by John Varner. Austin: University of Texas Press, 1981.

Velasco, Juan López de. *Geografía y descripción universal de las Indias.* Madrid: Estab. tip. de Fortanet, 1894.

Vignoles, Charles. *Observations upon the Floridas.* Brooklyn: E. Bliss and E. White, 1824.

Vollaro, Daniel. "Sixty Indians and Twenty Canoes: Briton Hammon's Unreliable Witness to History." *Native South* 2 (2009): 133–147.

Wallace, Antoinette B. "Native American Tattooing in the Protohistoric Southeast." In *Drawing with Great Needles: Ancient Tattoo Traditions of North America*, ed. Aaron Deter-Wolf and Carol Diaz-Granados, 1–42. Austin: University of Texas Press, 2013.

Waselkov, Gregory A., and Kathryn E. Holland Braund, eds. *William Bartram on the Southeastern Indians*. Lincoln: University of Nebraska Press, 1995.

Weber, David J. *The Spanish Frontier in North America*. New Haven: Yale University Press, 1992.

Weisman, Brent R. *Unconquered People: Florida Seminole and Miccosukee Indians*. Gainesville: University Press of Florida, 1999.

———. "Why Florida Archaeology Matters." *Southeastern Archaeology* 22 (2003): 210–226.

Wenhold, Lucy L., trans and ed. *A 17th Century Letter of Gabriel Díaz Vara Calderón, Bishop of Cuba, Describing the Indians and Missions of Florida*. Washington, DC: Smithsonian Institution, 1932.

Wentz, Rachel K. *Life and Death at Windover: Excavations of the 7,000 Year-Old Cemetery*. Cocoa: Florida Historical Society Press, 2012.

———. "The Origins of American Medicine." *Archaeology Magazine* (May/June 2011): 57–65.

Wentz, Rachel K., and John A. Gifford. "Florida's Deep Past: The Bioarchaeology of Little Salt Spring (8So18) and Its Place among Mortuary Ponds of the Archaic." *Southeastern Archaeology* 26 (2007): 330–337.

Wheeler, Ryan J. "Archaeology of Brickell Point and the Miami Circle." *FA* 53 (2000): 294–322.

———. "The Naples Canal: A Deep Indian Canoe Canal in Southwestern Florida." *FA* 51 (1998): 25–36.

———. *Southern Florida Sites Associated with the Tequesta and Their Ancestors* (NRHP Documentation Form). Tallahassee: Florida Division of Historical Resources.

Wheeler, Ryan J., and Robert Carr. "It's Ceremonial, Right?: Exploring Ritual in Ancient Southern Florida through the Miami Circle." In *New Histories of Pre-Columbian Florida*, edited by Neill J. Walls, 203–222. Gainesville: University Press of Florida, 2014.

Wheeler, Ryan J., James J. Miller, Ray M. McGee, Donna Ruhl, Brenda

Swann, and Melissa Memory. "Archaic Period Canoes from Newnans Lake, Florida." *American Antiquity* 68 (2003): 533–551.

White, David H. "The Spaniards and William Augustus Bowles in Florida, 1799–1803." *FHQ* 54 (1975): 145–155.

Whitfield, Stephen J. "Florida's Fudged Identity." *FHQ* 71 (1993): 413–435.

Wickman, Patricia Riles. *The Tree That Bends: Discourse, Power, and the Survival of Maskoki People.* Tuscaloosa: University of Alabama Press, 1999.

———. "'A Trifling Affair': Loomis Lyman Langdon and the Third Seminole War." *FHQ* 63 (1985): 303–317.

Widmer, Randolph J. "Archaeological Investigations at the Brickell Point Site, 8DA12, Operation 3." *FA* 57 (2004): 11–57.

———. *The Evolution of the Calusa: A Nonagricultural Chiefdom on the Southwest Florida Coast.* Tuscaloosa: University of Alabama Press, 1988.

Williams, John Lee. *The Territory of Florida or Sketches of the Topography, Civil and Natural History of the Country, the Climate, and the Indian Tribes from the First Discovery to the Present Time.* New York: A. T. Goodrich, 1837.

Wilmeth, Don B., and Christopher Bigsby. *Cambridge History of American Theater.* 3 vols. Cambridge: Cambridge University Press, 2008.

Wilson, Frederick Page. "Miami: From Frontier to Metropolis: An Appraisal." *Tequesta* 14 (1954) 25–49.

Wolfe, Patrick. "Settler Colonialism and the Elimination of the Native." *Journal of Genocide Research* 4 (2006): 387–409.

Wolfe, William A., and Janet B. Wolfe. *Names and Abstracts from the Acts of the Legislative Council of the Territory of Florida.* Pass-A-Grille Beach, FL: The Authors, 1985.

Wood, John Taylor. "Escape of General Breckenridge." In *Famous Adventures and Prison Escapes of the Civil War,* 295–311. New York: Century Company, 1893.

———. "Escape of the Confederate Secretary of War." *Century Illustrated Magazine* (November 1893): 110–123.

Woodward, C. Vann. *Origins of the New South, 1877–1913.* Baton Rouge: Louisiana State University Press, 1951.

Worth, John E. "Creolization in Southwest Florida: Cuban Fishermen and 'Spanish Indians,' ca. 1766–1841." *Historical Archaeology* 46, no. 1 (2012): 142–160.

———. *Discovering Florida: First-Contact Narratives from Spanish Expedi-*

*tions along the Lower Gulf Coast.* Gainesville: University Press of Florida, 2014.

———. "Fontaneda Revisited: Five Descriptions of Sixteenth-Century Florida." *FHQ* 73 (1995): 339–352.

———. "Razing Florida: The Indian Slave Trade and the Devastation of Spanish Florida, 1659–1715." In *Mapping the Mississippian Shatter Zone: The Colonial Indian Slave Trade and Regional Instability in the American South*, edited by Robbie Ethridge and Sheri Shuck-Hall, 295–311. Lincoln: University of Nebraska Press, 2009.

———. "Tracking the Calusa Overseas." *Friends of the Randell Research Newsletter* 1 (December 2002): 1.

Wright, E. Lynne. *More Than Petticoats: Remarkable Florida Women.* Guilford, CT: Morris Book Publishers, 2010.

Wright, J. Leitch, Jr. "Blacks in British East Florida." *FHQ* 54 (1970): 425–442.

———. *William Augustus Bowles, Director General of the Creek Nation.* Athens: University of Georgia Press, 1967.

Wynne, Nick, and Joe Crankshaw. *Florida Civil War Blockades: Battling for the Coast.* Charleston, SC: History Press, 2011.

Zeiller, Warren. *A Prehistory of South Florida.* Jefferson, NC: MacFarland and Company, 2005.

Zubillaga, Felix. *Monumenta Antiquae Floridae.* Rome: Monumenta Histórica Societatis Iesu, 1946.

# Index

Andrew K. Frank is the Allen Morris Associate Professor of History at Florida State University. He is the author of *Creeks and Southerners: Biculturalism on the Early American Frontier* as well as numerous other books and articles on the history of Florida and the southeastern Indians. He received his Ph.D. from the University of Florida.

FLORIDA IN FOCUS

Edited by Frederick R. Davis and Andrew K. Frank

Books in this series provide original and lively introductions to a range of topics in Florida history. Written by established scholars and using original research, the books draw upon current scholarly developments to situate subjects in a broad historical context.

*Before the Pioneers: Indians, Settlers, Slaves, and the Founding of Miami,* by Andrew K. Frank (2017)